The Last Days

Cycle C Sermons for
Proper 18 / Ordinary Time 23 / Pentecost 13
through Christ the King Sunday based
on the Gospel Texts

Richard Hasler

CSS Publishing Company, Inc.
Lima, Ohio

THE LAST DAYS
CYCLE C SERMONS FOR PROPER 18 / ORDINARY TIME 23 / PENTE-
COST 13 THROUGH CHRIST THE KING BASED ON THE GOSPEL TEXTS

FIRST EDITION
Copyright © 2018
by CSS Publishing Co., Inc.
Published by CSS Publishing Company, Inc., Lima, Ohio 45807. All rights
reserved. No part of this publication may be reproduced in any manner
whatsoever without the prior permission of the publisher, except in the
case of brief quotations embodied in critical articles and reviews. Inqui-
ries should be addressed to: CSS Publishing Company, Inc., Permissions
Department, 5450 N. Dixie Highway, Lima, Ohio 45807.

Library of Congress Cataloging-in-Publication Data
Names: Hasler, Richard A., author.
Title: The last days : Cycle C sermons for Proper 18, Ordinary Time 23,
    Pentecost 13 through Christ the King Sunday on the Gospel texts /
Richard Hasler.
Description: FIRST EDITION. | Lima : CSS Publishing Company, Inc.,
2019. | Includes bibliographical references and index.
Identifiers: LCCN 2018052113 (print) | LCCN 2018053865 (ebook) | ISBN
    9780788029233 (eBook) | ISBN 9780788029226 (pbk. : alk. paper)
Subjects: LCSH: Bible. Luke--Sermons. | Pentecost--Sermons. | Lection-
ary preaching. | Common lectionary (1992). Year C.
Classification: LCC BS2595.54 (ebook) | LCC BS2595.54 .H37 2019 (print)
| DDC   252 /.64--dc23

For more information about CSS Publishing Company resources, visit our website at www.csspub.com, email us at csr@csspub.com, or call
(800) 241-4056.

e-book:
ISBN-13: 978-0-7880-2923-3
ISBN-10: 0-7880-2923-1

ISBN-13: 978-0-7880-2922-6
ISBN-10: 0-7880-2922-3   PRINTED IN USA

Contents

Introduction   **5**

Proper 18 / Ordinary Time 23 / Pentecost 13   7
Luke 14:25-33
A Young Man's Vow

Proper 19 / Ordinary Time 24 / Pentecost 14   15
Luke 15:1-10
The Joy Of Being Found

Proper 20 / Ordinary Time 25 / Pentecost 15   23
Luke 16:1-13
The Dishonest Manager

Proper 21 / Ordinary Time 26 / Pentecost 16   29
Luke 16:19-31
Do You See Lazarus On Your Doorstep?

Proper 22 / Ordinary Time 27 / Pentecost 17   37
Luke 17:5-10
Small Beginnings, Great Endings

Proper 23 / Ordinary Time 28 / Pentecost 18   45
Luke 17:11-19
Where Are The Nine?

Proper 24 / Ordinary Time 29 / Pentecost 19   51
Luke 18:1-8
Persistence And Prayer

Proper 25 / Ordinary Time 30 / Pentecost 20   60
Luke 18:9-14
Two Contrasting Prayers

All Saints Day   66
Luke 6:20-31
The Gigantic Reversal

Proper 26 / Ordinary Time 31 / Pentecost 21   72
Luke 19:1-10
Out On A Sycamore Limb

Proper 27 / Ordinary Time 32 / Pentecost 22   80
Luke 20:27-38
A Trick *Resurrection*

Proper 28 / Ordinary Time 33 / Pentecost 23   88
Luke 21:5-19
Are We Living In The Last Days?

Christ the King Sunday (Proper 29)   96
Luke 23:33-43
A Last Appeal

Introduction

"People favor underdogs but follow top dogs. Fight for some underdogs anyway," wrote Kent M. Keith while at Harvard in 1968.

That is why I like Luke among the gospel writers because he tended to favor the underdogs.

Sermons On The Gospels; thirteen sermons for the "second half" after Pentecost, Cycle C, consists of sermons related to some of the last days of Jesus recorded in the gospel of Luke leading into Holy Week. This section covers a variety of topics: parables, prayer, the "end time" itself, and concludes with a believing criminal hanging on a cross next to Jesus who made his final request.

Luke, of all the four gospel writers, placed his emphasis upon the universality of the Christian gospel. He wrote for Gentiles as well as for the Israelites, the covenant people. He included "outsiders," such as women, children, the poor, aliens, strangers, and even a believing criminal upon the cross. Luke's story, probably written about 80 CE, or a few years before or after this date, accents the universality of the gospel. He had much to say about discipleship and eventually Luke's story leads us to Jesus' teaching about the "day of the Lord" and the end time. The author of this book is often identified as a physician and a traveling companion of the apostle Paul in his missionary journeys; however, some modern biblical commentators dispute this claim.

I want to thank a number of people who have assisted me in writing this book. First of all, David Runk, president and publisher of CSS who asked me to do this particular writing project and who provided keen insights that have made this book better than the original manuscript; Karyl Corson, project manager, who has guided me on this manuscript from beginning to end; Clare Coffee, head reference librarian, reference librarians, and other librarians at the Cuyahoga Falls, Ohio, Public Library; Janet Ross whose comments in Chapter 7 and Chapter 8 are especially poignant; Karen Kelly, my daughter whose computer expertise I rely upon frequently and who helped me in many different ways with this manuscript; and finally, my wife Arlene who is my unswerving inspiration, one who is constantly upbeat, encouraging me at all times. She has read the full manuscript making helpful suggestions and has added her own computer competence. Any errors of fact or interpretation are my own.

A Young Man's Vow

A young man awakens in the morning and hears the birds singing. He realizes how fortunate he is. It is summer time and he is back home in his father's parsonage in Gunsbach, Germany. Recently, he has been reading about Jesus' call in the gospels:

"Whoever does not carry the cross and follow me cannot be my disciple."

"From everyone to whom much is given, much will be required."

Whoever would save his life shall lose it, and whoever shall lose his life for my sake and the gospel shall save it."

What do these verses from the Bible mean?

This young university student, named Albert Schweitzer, decided that day Jesus' words had spoken to him personally. He had lived a privileged life. God had given him many gifts. What should be his response?

The young student resolved to continue his studies. He gained a doctorate in philosophy and later one in medicine. He was a yawningly brilliant student, and he planned to continue his academic studies until the age of thirty, when he would study medicine and become a physician. He came across a missionary magazine in 1904 and noticed that the Paris Missionary Society was looking for a missionary doctor to work in their Congo mission.

Schweitzer wrote in his autobiography: "My thirtieth birthday, a few months later, I spent like the man in the parable who 'desiring to build a tower, first counts the cost whether he have wherewith to complete it. The result was that I resolved to realize my plan of direct human service in Equatorial Africa."[1]

As he planned to enter the mission field, his family and close friends attempted to persuade him otherwise, telling him he would be wasting his enormous gifts in Africa. His wife, Helene, served as a nurse by his side for many years. Eventually, she had to leave him and return to Europe because of poor health. From time to time Dr. Schweitzer returned to Europe where he was honored for his achievements at Lambarene.

Schweitzer was not without his critics who complained about his primitive hospital and its poor sanitary conditions, but the African people loved him and continued to come to him for medical services. During World War II he was prohibited from traveling because of wartime conditions.

Schweitzer was noted for his organ music, especially for his mastery of Bach, but he also was acclaimed for his knowledge of the construction of the organ itself. For example, Pierre van Passen recalled, "How Dr. Schweitzer once came to Autopen (Holland) to preach the Christmas sermon when I was a guest at the manse. He arrived on a Monday and Christmas fell on a Saturday. We did not see the great man all week, until finally passing the cathedral and hearing the organ, we found Dr. Schweitzer covered with dust and sweat, up in the loft busy cleaning the pipes. On Christmas he not only preached the sermon, but also played the organ to the astonishment of the churchgoers who upon entering

1. Albert Schweitzer, *Out of My Life and Thought*, An *Autobiography: (New York: A Mentor Book, Henry Holt and Company, Inc., 1949), 70.*

the cathedral, looked up with amazement when they heard the prelude and said, 'Is that our old organ?' "[2]

In the scripture passage, Luke 14:26-33, Luke had Jesus speaking to the disciples and to the large crowds following him. These people were unaware that Jesus was going to Jerusalem not just to celebrate the Passover but also to die upon the cross. Jesus never pulled any punches, but he told them bluntly that they were not in it for a "joy ride." If they really wanted to be his disciples and not just followers, they should be prepared to suffer, and perhaps even die in following him.

Jesus undoubtedly shocked those who followed him to learn that they must "hate" their family. Ordinarily, Jesus exalted the family, but in this instance although loving our family was a legitimate loyalty, there was a loyalty that superseded loyalty to the family, namely loyalty to God. Did they realize what they were doing in following Jesus on this occasion? He was going to the cross and nothing was greater than what he was doing. Not family, not their possessions, not even their very lives.

Two stories Jesus told to illustrate what he had in mind, one involved building a "tower" the other pertained to preparing for "war." In a vineyard, the owner would build a tower so that he could see if thieves had invaded his vineyard and if roaming animals might be a threat. Likewise, when war was imminent; one did not prepare in a haphazard way, but rather took careful count of the size of the enemy and what it would take to overcome such numbers.

Did many of the people that followed him that day, really know what was involved? They were not going

2. Ibid.,191.

9

to a picnic, or even a celebration, but if they followed him they were going to a cross. The people seemed to be enthusiastic enough but for the wrong reasons. They were expecting a "joy ride." Jesus sought to correct this misapprehension. They didn't understand the seriousness of discipleship. He was going toward Jerusalem. It would be costly, even dangerous.

Tom Wright put it this way: He asked us to imagine we were on a serious expedition when our leader reminds us "that we are 'forging a way through a high and dangerous mountain pass to bring urgent medical aid to villagers cut off from the rest of the world.' 'If you want to come any further,' the leader says, 'you'll have to leave your packs behind, from here on the path is too steep to carry all that stuff. You probably won't find it again. And you'd better send your last postcards home' this is a dangerous route and it's very likely that several of us won't make it back.'"[3]

We may not like to hear these words, but we know why they must be said. Such was the situation in Jesus' day.

In our own time, no one has explained Christian discipleship better than the German theologian and pastor, Dietrich Bonhoeffer. In his book titled *The Cost of Discipleship* he explained what he means by "cheap grace" and "costly grace."

"Cheap grace is the preaching of forgiveness without requiring repentance and baptism without church discipline. Cheap grace is grace without discipleship, grace without the cross, grace without Jesus Christ, living and incarnate."

3. Tom Wright, *Luke for Everyone* (Louisville, Kentucky: Westminster John Knox Press, 2004), 180.

"Costly grace is the treasure hidden in the field; for the sake of it a man will gladly go and sell all that he has. It is the pearl of great price to buy which the merchant will sell all his goods. It is the kingly rule of Christ, for whose sake a man will pluck out his eyes which causes him to stumble; it is the call of Jesus Christ at which the disciple leaves his nets and follows him."[4]

We all want to be in control of our lives, believing that is what is best for us. But the opposite is really true. God is the one we should trust above all others.

Fred Buechner recalled a time in his life when everything seemed out of control, and he did not know what to do. "I remember sitting parked by the roadside once, terribly depressed, afraid about my daughter's illness and what was going on in our family, then out of nowhere a car came along down the highway with a license plate that bore on it the one word out of all of the words in the dictionary that I needed most to see exactly then. The word was *trust*.

Later on he learned that the owner of the car, as Buechner guessed, was a trust officer in a bank. Later, Buechner mentioned this incident in an article he had written. The trust officer traced his address and one day appeared on the doorstep with the license plate. Buechner now keeps the battered license plate on a bookshelf in his home "as holy a relic as I have ever seen."[5]

What does the Bible say? "Blessed is the one who trusts in the Lord, whose trust is in the Lord (Jeremiah

4. Dietrich Bonhoeffer, *The Cost of Discipleship* (New York: A Touchstone Book, Published by Simon & Schuster, 1995), 44-45.

5. George Connor, Compiler, *Daily meditation with Frederick* Buechner *(New York*, Harper San Francisco, *A Division of HarperCollins* Publishers, 1971), 326.

17:7). "When I am afraid, I will trust in you" (Psalm 56:3). "Cast all your anxiety on God because God cares for you" (1 Peter 5:7).

John Wesley made it a practice to recite the following pledge for forty years at the New Year's Eve Watch Night service:

I am no longer my own
        but yours.
Put me to what you will,
    rank me with whoever you will.
Put me to doing…
Put me to suffering.
    Let me be employed for you
    or laid aside for you
Exalted for you or
Brought low for you.
Let me be full
Let me be empty
    Let me have all things
    Let me have nothing!
And now O Father,
        You are mine and I am yours.
    So be it. And the covenant I am
making on earth,
    Let it be ratified in heaven.
Amen.[6]

We all have the need of wanting to be in control of everything. Perhaps we all would be better off if things were out of our control. We have seen that Wesley learned this lesson early in his career, and he reminded

6. Leonard Sweet, *A Cup of Coffee at the Soul Cafe* (Nashville: Broadman & Holman Publishers, 1998), 167.

himself at the beginning of each new year at the Watch Night service.

In the Bible we have the example of Abraham and Sarah going out from their home not knowing where they were going. David looked to the hills whence came his strength. Joshua and Caleb were not discouraged from their spying expedition in Canaan because the enemy looked bigger than the armies of Israel.

Closer to home, I once had the privilege of helping to lead a seminar for young pastors. The main leader was Phil, our executive presbyter. He had had a heart attack in the prime of life. During one of the discussion periods Phil shared what effect the heart attack had upon his ministry. His heart attack made him realize that he had been trying to do too many things at the same time all by himself. He finally decided, in his words, 'to resign as "the manager of the universe." Since then, he trusted God to control his life. He had peace when he came to realize that he did not have to accomplish everything by himself.

Albert Schweitzer, Fred Buechner, John Wesley, and Phil Bembower learned this lesson, and we must learn it too if we are to become true disciples of Jesus.

Amen.

The Joy Of Being Found

D. L. Moody tells the story somewhere of going to a jail to preach and when he began to preach he saw a sign in the back of the hall that read in large bold letters:

DO NOT PREACH ON THE PRODIGAL SON.

Apparently, the prisoners had had enough sermons on that particular parable, even though it is one of Jesus' most powerful parables about God's redeeming grace.

Fortunately, our lectionary text Luke 15:1-10 does not include the parable of the prodigal son. We do have two similar parables: the lost sheep and the lost coin that also speak of "The Joy Of Being Found."

Luke's image of the shepherd who leaves the ninety and nine sheep and goes seeking the one lost sheep is based upon several Old Testament passages:

"As shepherds seek out their flocks when they are among the scattered sheep, so I will seek out my sheep. I will rescue them from all the places to which they have scattered on a day of clouds and thick darkness" (Ezekiel 34:12).

"He will feed his flock like a shepherd; he will gather the lambs in his arms and carry them in his bosom, and gently lead the mother sheep"(Isaiah 40:11).

"Thus says the Lord God: I will soon lift up my hand to the nations, and raise my signal to the peoples; and they shall bring your sons in their bosom, and your daughters shall be gathered on their shoulders" (Isaiah 49:22).

Ira Sankey was D. L. Moody's song leader in the early days of his campaigns. One day, Sankey received a letter from Elizabeth C. Clephane with a poem tucked inside. Moody also received a letter addressed to him the same day.

Sankey wrote:

"I called Mr. Moody's attention to it, and he asked me to read it to him. This I proceeded to do with all the vim and energy at my command. After I finished I looked at Moody to see what the effect had been, only to discover he had not heard a word so absorbed was he in a letter he had received. I cut out the poem and placed it in my musical scrapbook.

"At the meeting on the second day, the subject was the good shepherd. At the conclusion Moody turned to me with the question: 'Have you a solo appropriate for this subject with which to close? I was troubled to know what to do. At this moment I seemed to hear a voice saying: 'Sing the hymn you found on the train!' But I thought this impossible, as no music had been written for it. Placing the newspaper slip on the organ, I lifted my heart in prayer, struck the key of "A" flat and began to sing.

"Note by note the tune was given, which has not been changed from that day to this, Mr. Moody was greatly moved. He came to where I was seated and said, 'Sankey where did you get this hymn? I never heard the like of it in my life.' Moved to tears, I replied,

'Mr. Moody, that's the hymn I read to you yesterday on the train, which you did not hear.'"[7]

That was the strange way in which the hymn "The Ninety and Nine" was first sung at a Moody revival meeting, a hymn based on our first parable.

As we seek to understand this first parable we must keep in mind the context in which it is written. Luke had just noted that the tax collectors and sinners were coming to listen to Jesus. Also, Jesus had eaten with such people. Therefore, Luke used this parable to show that God's love reaches out to even one tax collector or sinner who is away from the fold. Such is the amazing love of God that God is not content until all are safely in the fold. The Pharisees and scribes tended to put boundaries around people, certain ones were not included in their elect.

The Pharisees in particular would not defile themselves by associating with the so-called "people of the land" who did not observe the law, many of whom could not read or write, but Jesus loved them and associated with them nonetheless. Jesus identified with the shepherd image. In his day, the shepherd had a special responsibility for lost sheep. The shepherd was skilled in finding lost sheep, and if the worse happened to the lost sheep the shepherd had to bring home the fleece to show how the sheep had died.

We can imagine what the "people of the land" thought of Jesus' words, if they understood him correctly they didn't have to earn God's love. God was already coming looking for them and when they were found, a noisy celebration ensued.

7. Robert J. Morgan, *Then Sings My Soul: 150 of the World's Greatest Hymn Stories* (Nashville: Thomas Nelson Publishers, 2003), 171.

The following parables are quite similar in length, form, and content. Once again, no geographical reference is given. The Pharisees and scribes are critical of Jesus' eating habits, namely eating with tax collectors and sinners. In verse 7:38 Jesus was described as "Behold a glutton and a drunkard, a friend of tax collectors and sinners."

The first two parables are obviously twins, featuring a man and a woman. Note how they are joined together by the connection "or" in verse eight. Both of these parables are not found in Matthew and Mark. The Pharisees' concern was that Jesus was meeting with and even eating with, the wrong kind of people. The Pharisees were very strict in obeying the law of Moses, and they expected others to do the same.

Some students of the Bible have been critical of the shepherd for leaving the ninety and nine sheep in the wilderness unprotected. The emphasis here is to accent God's amazing love represented by the shepherd who diligently searches for the loss sheep at the risk of his own life.

In the second parable about the lost coin the woman also did not "give up" until she found it. Then when she found it she was filled with joy. She must tell others. She had a party. Her joy must not be kept to herself, but she must share it with someone else.

The first parable is about a lost sheep. Jesus said: "Which one of you having a hundred sheep and losing one of them, does not leave the ninety and nine in the wilderness and go after the one that is lost until he finds it?" (15:4).

What follows was a celebration. "When he has found it, he lays it on his shoulders and rejoices. And when he comes home, he calls together his friends and neighbors, saying to them, 'Rejoice with me, for I have found my sheep that was lost" (15:6).

Jesus concluded by saying: "Just so, I tell you, there will be more joy in heaven over one sinner who repents than over ninety-nine righteous persons who need no repentance (15:7).

The parable of the lost coin is similar to the first parable.

Jesus said: "Or what woman having ten silver coins, if she loses one of them, does not light a lamp, sweep the house, and search carefully until she finds it?" (15:8).

Once again a celebration ends this story. "When she finds it, she calls together her friends and neighbors, saying 'Rejoice with me, for I have found the coin I had lost '"(15:9).

Jesus concludes these two parables in a similar manner: "Just so, I tell you, there is joy in the presence of the angels of God over one sinner who repents" (15: 10).

Regarding the banquet itself, Tom Wright tells of an episode in his own life:

"We had just moved to a dream location: quiet, secluded, at the end of the road near a lake. Everything was peaceful. Then, on the first Saturday night we were there, all chaos broke loose. Loud music, amplified voices making announcements, cheers, fireworks — all going on well into the small hours, keeping our young children awake. We were appalled. Was this going to happen every weekend? Where was the noise coming from? Why had nobody told us about this before we bought the house?

In the morning, the explanations came. No, it wasn't a regular occurrence. It would only happen once a year. It was the local Yacht Club's annual party celebrating some great event in the sailing calendar. We returned to tranquility.

But it left me thinking about how one person's celebration can be really annoying for someone else, especially if they don't understand the reason for the party." [8]

There can be no doubt why the two people in our two parables were celebrating. They had told all their friends and neighbors; they were so happy that what they thought was lost had now been found.

Who are the "lost" people of our generation? Where are they? A young person wrote to her pastor to tell him where she had found such people.

Dear Max,

Last night I had an interesting experience that I would like to share with you,

I was at a place with lots of rooms — people gathering for all kinds of purposes.

One sign said "Christian Fellowship" so that's where I went.

The room was nearly packed and a lot of conversation was going on. I was drawn to a group where one young woman was really struggling. She was raised by and lives with a family of Satanists (unbelievable) but somehow Christ must have touched her because she was trying to find a way into the light. Since I was a latecomer, I don't know all her background — but a few people were talking to her and trying to help her. I joined in and was surprised to find myself witnessing

8. Tom Wright, *Luke for Everyone*, 183.

in this way — I'm usually too private about my faith (You know I don't wear that button out in the world.)... I am not great at quoting scripture but I do an okay job of sharing my experience with Christ so I figured God could do his work and I'd be willing. One of the people of the group was sort of the leader — I'm guessing he had some experience with this because he seemed to know when to move this girl forward.

The rest of us gave our "amens" and shared whatever we were inspired to add. We held hands, cried, prayed, and gave thanks ... eventually we were led in prayer by this girl and one and another turned their lives over to God...

There are more details to this story, but they aren't important to share at the moment. What I do want to share though is why I am writing this to you. I just wanted to let you know *Jesus is active in cyberspace.* Thought that you could appreciate that! (Yes what I am saying is that this all took place by way of computer.) If you are interested and the Spirit moves you, I am open to further discussion. Do you suppose that one day the church might support mission work out there in C—S? There are certainly a lot of lost searching souls there!

Have we thought about the internet being a mission field? Is it not true that so many people, especially our youth, are tied to their electronic screens of various kinds?

Amen.

The Dishonest Manager

When Robert Rubin (who eventually became trea-
sury secretary of the United States) as a high school
senior applied to Princeton and Harvard he received a
rejection letter from Princeton but he was accepted at
Harvard. He had hoped to go to Princeton. Four years
later Rubin sent a letter to the Director of Admissions
at Princeton saying: "You ought to be interested to
know what happened to one of the people you rejected
... I graduated from Harvard *summa cum laude and Phi
Beta Kappa.*"

Later, Rubin received a reply from Princeton's Director of Admissions: *"Every year at Princeton we at
Princeton feel it is our duty to reject a certain number of
highly qualified people so that Harvard can have some good
students too."*[9]

In Rubin's recent memoir, *In An Uncertain World*,
he made it clear that he felt no grudge against Princeton and his note was "tongue in cheek." I assume the
Princeton reply was "tongue in cheek" too.

Not a few biblical scholars feel certain that Jesus is
telling this parable in the same light. He couldn't possibly mean for us to take this parable on face value.
Admittedly, this is one of the most difficult of Jesus'

9. Robert Rubin and Jacob Weisberg, *In An Uncertain World* (New York:
   Random House, Division of Random House Inc., 2003), 59.

parables to understand. Perhaps, at the bottom of this parable is the question of how we use our money.

In this particular story the "dishonest steward" or manager was charged with squandering his land-owner's property. When he learned of the landowners' plans to fire him he went to his clients with a scheme to make the most of the situation. For example, he asked one client, "How much do you owe? The man replied, "a hundred jugs of oil." The manager said, "Take your bill, sit down quickly, and make it fifty." The manager asks another client, "How much do you owe? The man replied, a hundred containers of wheat." The manager said, "Take your bill and make it eighty." He reduced each bill considerably resulting in a lower payment for each one. When the landowner realized what the manager had done he praised the man because "he acted shrewdly."

The lesson to be drawn according to the teller of the story is that "the children of this age are more shrewd in dealing with their own generation than are the children of light. "First of all, note that the landowner himself might not be above suspicion. His manager was only charged with financial misconduct. It does not say in the story that the landowner made a complete investigation to see whether or not the "charge" was true. We only have the landowner's reply which in effect said, "He sure pulled a fast one on me."

The term "children of light" is found in other parts of the New Testament. John in his gospel focused on Jesus as the light: "While you have the light, believe in the light, so that you become children of the light" (John 12:36).

Paul used "children of the light" as Luke did: "For once you were darkness, but now in the Lord you are light. Live as children of the light" (Ephesian 5:8).

Paul also wrote: "For you are all children of light and children of the day; we are not of the night or of darkness" (1 Thessalonians 5:5).

The people in Jesus' parables are not perfect people — in fact the people Jesus associated with by and large were far from perfect. Did he not say that he came to call sinners to repentance, not the righteous?

The teller of the parable went on to say:

"Whoever is faithful in very little is faithful also in much; and whoever is dishonest in a very little is dishonest also in much" (16:10).

Our conscience should not operate on a percentage basis. If we tell the truth 60% of the time we are not honest. If we are dishonest in small things, we will be dishonest in large things too.

"Also, if then you have not been faithful with dishonest wealth, who will entrust you to the true riches? And if you have not been faithful of what belongs to another, who will give you what is your own?" (16:11-12).

We do not really own anything. If we are not faithful in our daily tasks how will we be able to handle in the future what is really ours?

Finally, we read in the parable:

"No slave can serve two masters; for he will either hate the one and love the other, or be devoted to one and despise the other. You cannot serve God and wealth" (16:13).

Conceivably today one could work several part-time jobs doing one on regular time and the other jobs in one's spare time. But a slave has no spare time. Like-wise, serving God is no part-time job. We either belong to God totally or not at all.

If we look at the biblical text closely we observe that both parables in chapter 16 begin with the same words, "There was a rich man…" In the first section the words are addressed to the disciples (v. 1). In the second section the words are addressed to the Pharisees (v. 14). The first part is a constructive use of money, whereas the second part is a view of money that is spiritually fatal.[10]

Luke had much to say about wealth and poverty in his gospel. For example in the following passages: the song of Mary (1:46-55), the sermons of John the Baptist (3:10-14), the prophecy of Isaiah (61:1-2) (4:16-30), blessings and woes (6:20-25), the parable of the rich fool (12;1-21), warnings against anxiety 12:22-31), advice to guests and hosts (14:7-14), and the two parables in chapter one.

At the conclusion of this parable Jesus said "the children of this age" were more shrewd than "the children of light." Could one meaning be that when the manager realized that he was about to be fired he did some serious thinking, something that apparently "the children of light" often did not do.

Too often as Christians we say, "I believe in God's revelation in the Bible, I live by faith; I don't live by reason like the rationalists I know do."

Scott Peck, a psychiatrist, in his book, *The Road Less Traveled & Beyond: Spiritual Growth in an Age of Anxiety* told the story about a patient named John who lived about a twenty-minute drive from the doctor's office.

10. Fred B. Craddock, *Interpretation: Luke, A Bible Commentary for Teaching and Preaching* (Louisville, Kentucky: John Knox Press, 1990), 189.

He visited his psychiatrist twice a week for four years. During the period he used up all his life savings in the process.

From time to time, John complained about the distance involved in seeing the doctor for his appointments. Therefore, Dr. Peck gave John a map with a shortcut he could take on his visits to see him. After six months into therapy John complained again how long it took him to drive to his appointment. Dr. Peck asked him if he took the shortcut. John replied that he had lost his map; then Dr. Peck gave him another one. Six months later he complained again, and Dr. Peck gave him another map.

Still later, the man complained again about the long distance of getting to the doctor's office. Dr. Peck had enough. He said to John, "We are going for a drive." When they had driven both routes, his regular one and then the shortcut, Dr. Peck pointed out to John that he lost ten minutes in the round trip visit to his office every time he went there. In other words, in terms of miles, he had driven he lost two thousand minutes the past two years. John had wasted three days of his life. In terms of miles he had driven twelve thousand miles out of his way to avoid taking that short cut. Eventually, John saw the "light" but even then he said, "I suppose the dominant motive in my life is to avoid change."[11]

Could this be one reason why "the children of light" were less shrewd than "the children of this age" that they don't take enough time for hard thinking?

Amen.

---

11. M. Scott Peck, M.D., *The Road Less Traveled and Beyond : Spiritual Growth in an Age of Anxiety* (New York: Simon & Schuster, 1997), 40-41.

Do You See Lazarus On Your Door-step?

Whenever I think of a rich man I think of Howard Hughes. He was not only extremely wealthy but also extremely eccentric. Hughes once bought a Las Vegas television station for little less than four million dollars simply because he wanted to watch cowboy movies all night, and this station had cowboy movies but not playing all night. Hughes wanted to watch them up until 6 a.m. That is what you do if you are an eccentric millionaire.[12]

Hughes has helped me to understand the rich man in Jesus' parable. The point of the parable is not a sweeping condemnation of wealth but rather a critique of the rich man's self-centered ways. He didn't even "see" the poor man Lazarus sitting on his doorstep.

Jesus' audience this time was not the twelve disciples but the Pharisees. Those who proclaim the so-called "prosperity gospel" can find some resemblance of it in the book of Deuteronomy where the writers of the book have God not only blessing war but blessing success in the marketplace as signs of God's favor. The Pharisees had this viewpoint in their theology, but before we go bashing Pharisees, we may have on the conservative or liberal side of the spectrum those we think

12. Peter Harry Brown and Pat H. Broeske, *Howard Hughes: The Untold Story* (New York: A Dutton Book, Penguin Group, 1996), 339.

who are "Pharisees." Before we condemn them we might first consider the "Pharisee within." If we press hard enough we might find what is most objectionable in our "Pharisee" might lodge within us too.

Some interpreters of this biblical passage see not one but two parables. The first one, or at least the first part of the parable (19:1-26) is found in a variety of forms among the rabbis; it is a common story in the ancient world.

In the second part of the story (vv. 27-31) we have a reversal of fortune. The rich man was in misery, and the poor man at the gate was at Abraham's side, an ancient Hebrew expression for 'being in heaven." Nonetheless, the rich man still saw Lazarus as someone who ought to serve him, someone who would "dip his finger and cool my tongue; for I am in agony in these flames." Abraham reminded him that once he had received good things and Lazarus had received evil things, but now Lazarus was the one being comforted. Even if the poor man wanted to, he would not have been able, because, according to this story, "a great chasm had been fixed" so that those who wanted to pass from here to there cannot do so, "no one can cross from there to us."

Then, forgetting himself for the moment, he remembered his five brothers at home. They should be warned so that they will not come to this place of torment. But Abraham countered saying: "They have Moses and the prophets, they should listen to them." Then, the rich man in desperation said to Abraham, "If someone from the dead would go to them they would repent." Abraham's reply was still the same, if they did not listen to Moses and the prophets, neither would they be convinced even if "someone rises from the dead."

Now, let us take a closer look at the rich man. He was described as being dressed in purple and fine linen who feasted sumptuously every day. He certainly was rich, but the story does not say that the rich man had a criminal record, nor does it say that he kicked Lazarus as he walked into the house. He might have been considered a model citizen by his close friends, one who even gave to charity and watched the latest shows on PBS. In many respects he might have been considered a "good guy" in his time. But he did not "see" Lazarus on his doorstep.

Now, we take a look at the poor man, named Lazarus. Incidentally, this is the only parable of Jesus where the central figure of the story is given a formal name. Lazarus means "God is my help." He was described as a poor man sitting on the doorstep of the rich man. He was covered with sores. He was constantly hungry and begged for the crumbs that were dropped from the rich man's table. We also are told that the dogs of the street came and licked his sores.

Keith F. Nickel in his commentary on Luke has this rather lengthy summary:

"Luke surely expected his community to connect the conclusion of this story with the church's proclamation of Jesus' death and resurrection. The testimony of the Jewish scriptures was still true, yet Luke's colleagues in the faith had experienced people who would believe neither the testimony of scripture nor the witness of Christians to the good news that God had raised one from the dead who not only by his words but by his life demonstrated that God was dead serious about obedience.

Even more pointedly, the story converged with their own inclinations to equivocate. They too had Moses and the prophets; they even had the witness of the greatest of them all, John the Baptist; they had the testimony of Jesus' preaching of the good news of the restored rule of God; they had the Easter proclamation of Jesus raised by God from the dead. How thoroughly had it been taken? How single-minded were they in their willingness to place their trust exclusively in God? How consistent were they in relying on God alone, wherever they were, whatever happened, no matter what? How about us?"[13]

Tom Wright brought the story up to the present where it involves all of us "rich" people, in case we forget, by almost any human standard we in the United States are "rich"people in contrast to the rest of the world's population. Wright commented: "We have all seen him. He lies on a pile of newspapers outside a shop's doorway covered with a rough blanket. Perhaps he has a dog with him for safety. People walk past him, or even step over him. He occasionally rattles a few coins in a tin or cup, asking for more. He wasn't there when I was a boy, but he's there now, in all our cities, east, west, north, and south.

As I see him, I hear voices, "it's his own fault," they say. He's chosen it. There are agencies to help him. He should go and get a job. If we give him money he'll only spend it on drink. Stay away — he might be violent. Sometimes, in some places, the police will move him on, exporting the problem somewhere else. But he'll be back, and even if he isn't, there are whole societies

13. Keith Nickel, Preaching the Gospel of Luke: *Proclaiming God' Royal Rule (Louisville, Kentucky: Westminster John Knox Press, 2000), 169-170.*

like that. They camp in tin shacks on the edges of large, rich cities. From the door of their tiny makeshift shelters, you can see the high-rise hotels and office blocks where, if they're very lucky, one member of the family might work as a cleaner. They have been born into debt and in debt they will stay, through the fault of someone rich and powerful who signed away their rights, their lives in effect, a generation or two ago, in return for arms, a new presidential place, a fat Swiss account, and even if rich and poor don't always live side by side so blatantly, the television brings us together."[14]

Yes, we have all seen Lazarus many times, but have we really "seen" him?

We must always remember this is a parable, a story with "picture language" about something going on in Jesus' ministry. We must not take all the details literally but probe to the essential message. The rich man never really "saw" the poor man.

Annie Dillard, in her Pulitzer Prize winning book, *Pilgrim at Tinker Creek*, told stories of people blind from birth or people who had lost their sight for a long time. *"Finally, a 22-year-old girl was dazzled by the world's brightness and kept her eyes shut for two weeks. When at the end of that time she opened her eyes again, she did not recognize any objects, but the more she now directed her gaze upon everything about her, the more it could be seen how an expression of gratification astonishment overspread her features; she repeatedly exclaimed 'Oh God! How beautiful!' How we should praise God, if we can really see!"*[15]

We may see two lovers say "sweet nothings" to each other. We may even say, "I don't know what she

14. Tom Wright, *Luke for Everyone*, 199-200.

15. Annie Dillard, *Pilgrim at Tinker Creek* (New York: Harper Collins Publishers, 1998), 31.

sees in him." But the parties involved see things differently. As the lyrics in Sheldon Hanrick's song in *Fiddler on the Roof* exclaimed that of all of God's miracles, no matter the size, the most miraculous is the gift of one person to another.

In Rob Bell's book, *Love Wins*, he has a chapter on hell. In this chapter he talked about all kinds of hell. He discussed the rich man in the parable ignoring his neighbor. He contended that if enough rich men treated Lazarus outside their gates like that, it could conceivably lead to a widening gap between the rich and the poor and would eventually mean we would have an "individual" hell and a "societal" hell too.

Bell also discussed the scriptural passages that never mention the word "hell" but seem to be talking about it nonetheless. For example, take the story of Sodom and Gomorrah in chapter 19 of the book of Genesis. The judgment upon that city because of its sinfulness involved sulfur raining down from the heavens destroying all the living including even the vegetation of the land. Since that time Sodom and Gomorrah has become a sign of God's swift and certain judgment.

But is that the last we hear of Sodom and Gomorrah? In Ezekiel 16:53 we read: "I will restore the fortunes of Sodom and her daughters... Sodom and her daughters shall return to their former state." The story isn't over for Sodom and Gomorrah.

Also, in the New Testament we read in Matthew 10:15 speaking of the town the disciples may be visiting: "Truly I tell you, it will be more tolerable for Sodom and Gomorrah on the day of judgment than for that town." Bell went on to say: "More bearable for Sodom and Gomorrah?" He told highly committed, pious, religious people that it would be better for Sodom and Gomorrah than for them on the judgment day? And if there's still hope for Sodom and Gomorrah, what does that say about all of the other Sodoms and Gomorrahs?[16]

We can agree with Bell when he stated that the dominant theme of the Bible is healing and restoration. God judges in order to discipline, correct, and eventually restore.

We don't want to give up on the Lazarus on our doorstep or anyone else. God's compassionate grace continually seeks us.

Amen.

---

16. Rob Bell, *Love Wins: A Book about Heaven, Hell, and the Fate of every Person* (New York: Harper One, An Imprint of Harper Collins Publishers, 2011), 83-93.

Proper 22 / Ordinary Time 27 / Pentecost 17
Luke 17:5-10

Small Beginnings, Great Endings

On the day Abraham Lincoln was born his older
cousin Dennis Hanks went over to see the newborn
baby. Later he commented:
"Folks often ask me if Abe was a good-looking
baby. Well, he looked just like any other baby — like a
red cherry pulp squeezed dry, and he didn't improve
none as he growed older."[17]
That may be a typical cousin's reaction, but admittedly, Lincoln never was photogenic and he probably
would not have made it in this age of television with
all its glitz and style. Nonetheless, it is the considered
opinion of our nation's professional historians every
time a poll is taken Lincoln rates as the greatest president of the United States. From these humble and
unpromising beginnings, something great happened.
Small things do make a difference.

Our biblical passage, Luke 17:5-10, actually contains
four distinct sayings of Jesus on four different topics:
causing temptations, forgiveness, faith, and obedience.

Jesus' first saying regarded placing a temptation in
place of "little ones" — a phrase that usually means
those young in the faith. Jesus showed the seriousness

17. Philip B. Kunhardt, Jr, Philip B. Kunhardt III. and Peter Kunhardt,
    Lincoln: An Illustrated Biography (New York: Alfred A. Knopf, Inc.,
    1992), 35.

37

of this dying by giving a rather vivid picture of the offender having a millstone around his neck and then being tossed into the sea.

The second saying involves forgiveness. Even within the people of faith it is possible for disciples to sin. If this happens there is need for forgiveness on the part of the one offended, even if this happens seven times. There should be no limit to the forgiveness.

The third saying is on faith, the heart of this particular sermon. We will elaborate more on this topic later.

The fourth saying concerns the matter of obedience. A slave in this parable even though he had labored in the field all day long, should not feel that his work was done. He may say to himself, "Now is my time to eat and be served by someone else, but Jesus says that his servants should see the situation differently. He has domestic responsibilities and must serve the master first before eating himself.

Back to the third issue of "faith," which is our main concern today. We may wish to become mature Christians overnight, but spiritual growth takes time just as it does in the world of education and of nature.

Mustard seeds are not considered the smallest seeds in the Near East, as it is often claimed, but the mustard seed is tiny and eventually grows into a large plant or tree. Furthermore, birds are fond of the little seeds, and a cloud of birds over a mustard plant is a common sight. In the Hebrew scripture this image of the birds flocking to the trees was often used by the biblical writers as a sign of God's great coming kingdom. For example, in Ezekiel 17:23,"In the shade of its branches, the birds of every sort will nest" the prophet looks forward to that day of God's great coming kingdom. It was the grand dream of the Hebrew prophets that someday God's kingdom would include not only the covenant people of Israel but the Gentiles too, that is all the other nations of the world.

After hearing the first two sayings of Jesus is it any wonder that the disciples should ask, "Increase our faith"? Jesus countered by saying: "If you had faith the size of a mustard seed you could say to this mulberry tree, 'Be uprooted and planted in the sea, and it would obey you'"(17:6).

Matthew and Mark in their telling of Jesus' saying used the word "mountain" instead of "mulberry tree" but the result is the same: God has a way of doing the impossible if there is sufficient faith. More correctly, what is needed is not greater faith but simply faith in a great God. When we have this kind of faith we are attached to a power that can do anything.

In this third saying, Luke has Jesus giving a kind of "show and tell" lesson of the tiny mustard seed and its potential to reach numerous people around the world.

As we sit in the congregation in worship today we may not be aware of the dynamic possibility for change and growth in our individual lives and in the church as a whole. All God needs is a beginning, however small. Our Lord can take small beginnings and change them into great endings.

Our particular congregation in northeast Ohio has a practice on Rally Day as we begin a new year in the fall. At the end of the worship service, the whole congregation adjourns to the parking lot behind the church building to participate in a balloon contest. Each person, young and old, is given a balloon to send up into the sky to see how far their balloon can possibly go. My balloon did not go very far because it became entangled in the wires above the parking lot. My wife had a different experience with her balloon. Her balloon escaped the wires and continued on its way toward Pittsburgh. Attached to each balloon was a note identifying the church, the name and address of the sender, and a scriptural blessing for anyone who might find the balloon.

We waited and waited and soon reports came in from people who had found some of the balloons. In the case of my wife's balloon about two or three weeks later we received a letter from a young couple in Rochester, New York. Their letter told how much they enjoyed receiving it. It seems that they had been hiking in a state park just north of Pittsburgh and found the balloon and note there. It was a small gesture but was much appreciated.

How does spiritual growth happen? First of all, in understanding the dynamics of growth we need *patience.*

When James Garfield was president of Hiram College in Northeast Ohio (later he would become president of the United States), he was approached by a father of a boy seeking admission to the college. The father asked Garfield, "Can't you simplify the course? My boy will never be able to take all that in. He should be able to go through a shorter route."

"Certainly," Garfield replied, "I believe I can arrange that. Of course, it all depends upon what you want to make of your boy. When God wants to make an oak tree, he takes a hundred years. When he wants to make a squash, he requires only two months."[18] The most important things in life cannot be hurried.

18. Harold Kohn, *Pathways to Understanding: Outdoor Adventures in Meditation* (Grand Rapids, Michigan: Wm. B. Eerdmans Publishing Company, 1958), 113.

Nelson Mandela had to wait in prison for 27 years before his hope for a new South Africa could be achieved. In 1996, he saw the future of South Africa in its children when he dedicated a Children's Village in Capetown. He called for patience: "It is my hope that within this community a culture of understanding, acceptance, and love can be nurtured. Let this Children's Village be an example of tolerance and reconciliation so that we, as adults, can learn from these children."[19]

In the world of nature we note the sun rising and setting in its good time. In winter we wish that the warm weather would come, but we cannot force it. In the fall we long for the coming of the colorful warblers, but we cannot hurry them. They migrate when they will.

Likewise, within our own lives, God is at work within us, leading the way toward a specific objective. God is at work within us as a child, as a youth, and into our adult years even though we may not always be aware of his presence and direction.

Patience is needed in dynamic spiritual growth, but something else is needed too. We might call it *cooperation*.

We cannot compel growth to happen, but we can cooperate with it. Think of our own gardens, we plant seeds, water the soil, fertilize the ground, provide light and shade, prune, and control weeds.

Likewise, we can grow in our spiritual life, if we cooperate. We do this by using "means of grace", that includes regular worship, constant prayer, regular Bible reading, and serving others. These are "seeds" that

19. Nelson Mandela, *In His Own Words* (New York: Little, Brown and Company, 2003), 432.

God uses to effect change in our lives. Only God can really alter our lives, but we can cooperate.

Leo Buscaglia has often been called "the love doctor" for his emphasis upon love and his belief in the potential of every human being. He said that no one can count on what he is going to say. He prides himself in his unpredictability as a professor. He cooperates with the growth process. "When my students raise their hands and say, 'That isn't what you said Tuesday.' I say, 'I know I've grown since Tuesday. Do you expect me to be last Tuesday's Leo today?"[20] Buscaglia cooperated by improving himself from week to week.

Spiritual growth involves patience, cooperation, and finally what I call *surrender.* We must give up our old ways and seek something radically new. To be blunt, we must plant seeds, die, and wait for resurrection.

Literary scholars often consider the Russian novelist Feodor Dostoevsky's greatest novel to be *The Brothers Karamazov.* What interested me most about this novel was its scriptural epigraph attached to the book. It is John 24: "Verily, verily I say unto you, except a corn of wheat fall into the ground and die, it abideth alone: but if it die, it bringeth forth much fruit." (KJV)

Eugene Peterson, pastor, scholar, and translator, took time off from his pastoral schedule as a young mission pastor in Maryland to study the writings of Dostoevsky in depth, and he wrote of this experience with perception.

Dostoevsky had a troubled personal life. His marriage was in shambles. He gambled compulsively. His epilepsy crippled his writings. But he created. He

20. Leo Buscaglia, Ph.D., *Living, Loving, & Learning* (New York: Fawcett Columbine, published by Ballantine Books, 1982), 164.

planted seeds. He lived expecting that God would do something in his life. He was passionate in his relationship with God. He believed he could create nothing significant unless he depended upon God's grace working silently, patiently in his own life. "He planted seeds. Then he died to his aims and wishes. He waited for resurrection. And it came. We benefit immensely today in reading his works. They are filled with pain, disappointment, and anguish of everyday living but also with example after example of those who died to an old way of life only to find God has something better for them. But such transforming power can only happen if we are in touch with God." [21]

If we depend solely upon ourselves, we will not grow spiritually, but if we keep in contact with what Dostoevsky calls "other mysterious worlds" we will grow indeed. Many people prefer to glide through life with little effort, and they may think we are crazy to attempt the hard work of spiritual growth, but we must not be turned away from our goal.

Amen.

21. Eugene Peterson, *Under the Unpredictable Plant: An Exploration in Vocational Holiness* (Grand Rapids, Michigan: William B. Eerdmans Publishing Company, 1992), 66-67.

Where Are The Nine?

The mother of a little boy questioned him, "Why didn't you pray last night like you usually do?" His frank response was, "I didn't want anything from God last night." But is prayer only petition and intercession? Surely, "thanksgiving" is an integral part of prayer.

People in Jesus' time were threatened by leprosy, even more than we are today by the advent of AIDS. Definite regulations had been set up for the Jewish community to protect themselves from coming in contact with lepers. For example, in Leviticus 13:45-46:

"The person who has the leprous disease shall wear torn clothing and let the hair of his head be disheveled; and he shall cover his upper lip and cry out, "unclean, unclean." He shall remain unclean as long as he has the disease; he is unclean. He shall live alone: his dwelling shall be outside the camp."

When a band of lepers met others while walking, they must call out that they were lepers, and some ancient authorities said in the first century that at least fifty yards of distance must separate lepers from ordinary people.

Although lepers were not given much hope in biblical times, Jesus had compassion for them and gave them hope. In our scripture for today, Jesus healed all the lepers in the band, and then he told them to go to the priest to be examined. If found clean they would be admitted into the camp and into normal society.

All ten had been healed, but only one returned to thank Jesus. In keeping with Luke's emphasis upon the universality of the gospel, he has the one returning, a Samaritan. The Jews and the Samaritans were bitter enemies; the common cause that brought them together was the fact that they all were lepers.

It may seem strange to us that Jesus would send a Samaritan to a Jewish priest in order to be certified that he was cleansed from leprosy. Fred Craddock, New Testament scholar, seeks to resolve this problem by suggesting that what we have here are two stories: a healing story and a story of the salvation of a foreigner.[22]

Keith Nickel in his commentary on the gospel of Luke added another insight: "'Your faith has made you well' (v. 19) refers to more than the cleansing. It encompasses the discernment of the presence of the rule of God that brought the Samaritan back in glad and joyful celebration as a kingdom participant. 'Rise' means more than 'get up.' It alludes to participation in resurrection life..."[23]

Here we have a picture of human ingratitude. Jesus cured ten lepers, but only one came back to thank him. Often God helps us in a special way, but we too often forget to thank God for divine gifts.

Most of us here today have been born in the United States. If we had been born in Haiti, in Somalia, or in Iraq — how different would our lives be right now?

22. Fred B. Craddock, *Interpretation: Luke, A Bible Commentary for Teaching and Preaching*, 202-203.

23. Keith Nickel, *Preaching The Gospel of Luke: Proclaiming God's Royal Rule*, 177.

There is nothing we did to be born in the United States. It was a gift. Most of us were born in homes where we have love and support. We could have been born in a home where no one cared for us, where we would have had to somehow survive on our own.

Allen Emery, the author of the delightful little book titled, *A Turtle on the Fencepost*, argued that if you see a turtle on a fencepost you can be pretty sure that the turtle did not get there by itself. If that turtle brags about getting there itself, we know it is lying.

As people of faith we give thanks and give credit to the one who has put us where we are. We are extravagantly grateful but we express our gratitude in a variety of ways.

Our gratitude often reflects our unique personalities.

Brant Baker in his book, *P.R.A.Y.E.R.: Guidance for Church Leaders*, teaches others how to teach prayer to those for whom they have a responsibility. He mentioned Isabel and David Kersey, good Catholics as they are and how they have used outstanding Catholics in history to show a variety ways this might be done. In a rather fascinating way using the different personality types represented in the Myers-Briggs Type Indicator they show how people pray in different ways according to their personalities.

The first prayer mentioned is the *Thomistic Prayer*. This type of prayer is "logical; enjoys mental challenges, tends to rearrange environment (organizers); leaders, perfectionists, critical, demanding, likely to schedule even play time; communication tends to be precise, with a reluctance to state the obvious; straightforward; future oriented; desire for competency."

The second type of prayer is what they call the *Ignatian Prayer.*

This second type of prayer "wants to feel useful; typical of givers, rather than receivers; practical; work ethics; strong sense of tradition; conscientious; can be pessimistic — "If I don't do it who will?'; tends to enjoy ceremony and ritual; typical of great law and order people; careful, cautious, accurate; industrious; and always prepared."

The third type of prayer is called the *Augustinian Prayer.*

The characteristics of their prayers: "usually creative, optimistic, verbal; persuasive; outspoken great need for self-expression; tends to communicate with others easily; typical of good listeners; hates conflict, prefers face-to-face encounters; deep feelings; committed to helping others; compassionate; enthusiastic; always searching for meaning, authenticity, and self-identity; natural rescuers."

The final type of prayer is the *Franciscan Prayer.*

This prayer is "free; unconfined; impulsive; dislikes being tied down to rules; loves action; easily bored with the status quo; crisis-oriented; good trouble-shooters; flexible; open-minded; adaptable; willing to change position; tend to live very much in the present; dislikes practice and prefers to 'just do it.'"[24]

Do you fit into one of these four categories when you pray and express your gratitude to God? It is good to be aware of different personality types since we all don't express prayer and thanksgiving in the same way, even though we may be as authentic as the next person.

24. Brant D. Baker, *Teaching P.R.AY.E.R: Guidance for: Pastors and Church Leaders* (Nashville: Abingdon Press, 2001), 105-109.

Our gratitude may have a tinge of humor in it. Desmond Tutu imagines what would happen if Mary had been unresponsive to be the mother of Jesus:

"Knock, knock, come in. Yes Mary, God would you like to be the mother of his Son? What? Me? In this village you can't even scratch yourself without everybody knowing about it! You want me to be an unmarried mother? I'm a decent girl, you know. Sorry, try next door." [25]

Fortunately, we know Mary did not respond this way.

Our gratitude may be as simple as the privilege of watching the birds. Robert Raines, the director of Kirkridge, a retreat center in the heart of the resplendent Pocono Mountains of Pennsylvania has this explanation:

"I delight in a daily blessedness that visits me each morning in the wild birds at our feeders. Since 1978 we have had a bird log registering residents and visitors like rose-breasted grosbeaks, scarlet rangers, indigo buntings, and other outrageous birds who arrive annually during the first two weeks in May. Yes, I'm bragging, really celebrating the gorgeous invasion of the merry, merry month of May... We do not tire of watching cardinals appearing at dawn and dusk, or hearing the distant tom-tom sound that the pillaged woodpecker makes as it rat-a-tats a dead tree in the forest." [26]

Finally, our core gratitude to God may be all that might be required. Meister Eckhart, the Christian

25. Desmond Tutu, *God Has A Dream: A Vision of Hope for Our Time* (New York: Doubleday, a division of Random House, 2004), 61.

26. Robert Raines, *A Time to Live: Seven Tasks of Creative Aging* (New York: A Dalton Book, published by the Penguin Group, 1977), 71.

mystic, once wrote that "if the only prayer we ever prayed our whole life was 'Thank you' that would be enough."[27]
Amen.

27. Wayne Muller, *Sabbath: Finding Rest, Renewal, and Delight in Our Busy Lives* (New York: Bantom Books, 1999), 128.

Proper 24 / Ordinary Time 29 / Pentecost 19
Luke 18:1-8

Persistence And Prayer

"Abraham Lincoln once told a story about a blacksmith who stuck an iron bar in the coals until it was red hot. Then on the anvil, he pulled at the iron intending to make a sword. He was dissatisfied with the end product and put it back into the hot coals determined this time to make a garden tool. Once again, he was not pleased with what he had; therefore he tried making a horse shoe. That too did not please his fancy.

"As a last resort, he put the iron bar in the hot coals one more time. He removed it from the fire wondering if there was anything he could make from it. Deciding that there was nothing he merely stuck it into a barrel of water. At the resulting hiss, he said, 'Well, at least I made a fizzle out of it.'" [28]

Our dreams often do not turn out the way we have planned but maybe we can at least make a fizzle out of them.

The widow in our parable for today represented the poor people of the land in the time of Jesus. They had little protection against the leaders of society; in particular, this cruel judge would not listen to her pleas at first. The judge represented those in power who had

28. Robert Schuller, *Tough Times Never Last, But Tough People Do* (Nashville: Thomas Nelson Publishers, 1983), 91-92.

authority to do whatever they thought was right. More than likely he would not have been a Hebrew judge.

It was customary in the first century if a Jew had a complaint it was decided not by one judge but by a group of elders. This particular judge probably had been selected by King Herod to take the case of the widow. Such judges were normally corrupt, and he probably expected a bribe, which the poor widow was not able to pay. But the widow was persistent, so persistent that eventually the judge decided to hear her case rather than be continually pestered by her. Jesus was talking about prayer in this story. He definitely was not saying that God eventually would get tired of our constant prayers and give in to us. On the contrary, Jesus is saying just the opposite. He was setting up the judge to be the opposite of how God answers prayer. If the widow could wear down the judge by her persistence, Jesus was saying in this story how much more God will be willing to answer our prayers in contrast to this judge's action.

Of course, we often think that we need something when we do not need it now, at least not in the next hour, or in the next week, month, or year. Only God knows what is best for us in the long run. That is why Jesus says we must never be discouraged in prayer. Jesus wondered if the people of faith could stand to wait and endure the long delays until the coming of the son of man?

By the time Luke wrote his gospel apparently Jesus' followers were encountering resistance and possibly outright persecution. They were looking forward to the day of the Lord when God would make everything right. The fact that that day had not arrived did not mean that God did not care for them. This parable was given to them that they might not "lose heart" but should always be confident that the day of the Lord would come "quickly," that is in God's own time.

Various people have suffered in one way or another because of discrimination or various kinds of violence. The following examples illustrate this dissimilarity.

Domestic Violence — Janet Ross

In the congregation where my wife, Arlene, and I worship today, and where I served as a part-time associate pastor for five years, in my "retirement" it was decided by the pastoral staff to expand our worship services from two traditional services that we had each Sunday morning to include a brief contemporary service from 11:59 a.m. to 12:30 p.m.; hence, having all three services begin Sunday morning. The third service contained informal prayers, a brief meditation, and music that include old gospel hymns, jazz, and African-American spirituals. One of the soloists and song leaders in the third service was Janet Ross. Her thrilling voice made the music come alive. Although she was white the fact that she had experienced domestic violence as a young girl enabled her to identify with the spirituals of the black tradition.

Janet was a versatile person. She had a Doctor of Ministry degree in preaching from Chicago Theological Seminary; she had been a leader in inter-faith dialogue. She also had with her husband, Joel, a Fair Trade store that sold crafts and other items made in Haiti. Just recently she had been called part-time to be the preacher of the Amistad Chapel at the national headquarters of the United Church of Christ in Cleveland, Ohio.

The Reverend Doctor Janet Ross sang all the spirituals with an emotional exude that you just knew was authentic. One song I recall very well was "I Want Jesus to Walk with Me."

I have Janet's permission to quote from the following email:

> *"There always are multiple layers going on in my head when I sing spirituals. First of all, I'm always aware that I'm singing music from the African-American tradition. There is always this context running in my head, in my soul, that I'm singing music that was born out of their context. I stand in awe of the grace of a people who would adopt and adapt the religion of those who hurt and abused them — make truth telling complex, beautiful music out of that experience."[29]*

A black minister spoke to other people gathered to discuss racial prejudice and discrimination: "Until you have stood for years knocking at a locked door, your knuckles bleeding, you do not really know what prayer is."[30]

The black people of America have suffered much, not only during the years of slavery but also in more recent times with segregation and rampant racial discrimination.

How important it is for white people to have not just an intellectual knowledge of what the spirituals are about, but also "feel" what this black music is trying to convey.

Janet has that sense of "feeling" that many of the rest of us seemingly do not have. It is essential that we

29. Email conversation, November 21, 2015 with Janet Ross.

30. Fred B. Craddock, *Interpretation: Luke, A Bible Commentary for Teaching and Preaching*, 210.

capture the sensation of what the slaves really meant and felt when they wrote the spirituals.

Jewish Holocaust — Elie Wiesel

Elie Wiesel was certainly one who suffered immensely. He knew what it was to be persistent, just like the African-American slaves enduring their bondage in America. As a young Jewish teenager he was imprisoned by the Nazi in the infamous Auschwitz and Buchenwald concentration camps. In 1945, at the age of fifteen, at the close of World War II he was rescued. His parents and young sister were not so fortunate. They were the victims of the unspeakable horror of the holocaust. It was Wiesel, incidentally, who coined the term "holocaust" or "burnt offerings." He wanted to sear into the memory of people throughout the world that the cruelty that exterminated an estimated six million Jews must never happen again. Wiesel has turned his personal hell into a lesson for the whole world in the hope that we can learn from such agony. His more than twenty-five books during the past thirty years have had this one theme — hate mongers should have no place in society no matter who their targets may be.

Wiesel in his novel, *Night,* tells of his experience in the concentration camps. The story begins with Elie peacefully living in his village of Sighet, Hungary when suddenly the Nazi came. The Jews were restricted from leaving the ghetto, forced to wear a yellow star, and then they were deported, going to a place of which they had never heard. They were compelled to run faster and faster. They were jammed into railroad cars, eighty people to a car. The Gestapo officers treated them like cattle being herded into the railroad cars.

One woman sealed in at the car, where Elie and his father happened to be, went out of her mind screaming "Fire! Fire I can see the fire." Fellow Jews bound and gagged her to give everyone some peace. Finally, they arrived at their destination: Auschwitz. They had never heard of it.

Having arrived at the concentration camp, they were divided into groups, some went to the crematory, other to the workhouse. The women also were separated from the men. Elie's mother and young sister — he never saw again. Sick bestial brutality he had never seen before. He was coerced to walk naked carrying only his belt and shoes. In a book of a little more than a hundred pages he depicted the horrors of the camp.

Elie was transferred by train from Auschwitz to Buchenwald. His father died on the train. Three days after his liberation Elie became seriously ill with food poison, lingering between life and death. Having progressed a bit in his recuperation at the hospital, he wanted to see himself in the mirror. He recorded the sight he beheld:

"One day I was able to get up, after gathering all my strength, I wanted to see myself in the mirror hanging on the opposite wall.

From the depths of the mirror, a corpse gazed back at me. The look in his eye, as they stared into mine, has never left me."[31]

Now let us look at World War II from a different perspective, namely from the point of view of a German officer who participated in this horrible war. Lewis B. Smedes who taught at Fuller Theological Seminary for

31. Elie Wiesel, *Night* (translated from the French by Marion Wiesel, New York: Hill and Wang, A Division of Farrar, Straus and Giroux, 1958.

many years called our attention to Michael Christopher's powerful play called *The Black Angel*. The story was about a former German officer who tried to rebuild his life after World War II by hiding in the woods just outside a small French village. He had already paid the price for his awful involvement in purging the enemy of Germany, namely the French. The Nuremberg trials had sentenced him to thirty years in prison. Having served his term, he and his wife sought to live out their remaining few years hiding in the forest.

But a French journalist named Morrieu could not forget what happened. He remembered that in this tiny French village Nazi soldiers under the command of Engle had killed the villagers. Morris went back to the village and reminded the remaining people what had happened and that Engle and his wife were hiding in the woods, not far from the village. Their ire having been stimulated, the villagers decided to attack Engle and his wife that night.

Morrieu wanted to hear more details of the story. He still had some questions to ask Engle. He found him in the woods and began to interrogate him. He wanted to hear the details of the story. As the afternoon wore on Morrieu's taste for revenge lessened. For the first time, after thirty years he began to doubt that he knew the whole story. He changed his mind and told the frightened couple that the villagers planned this very night to come into the woods and kill them. Morrieu offered to lead them to safety.

The German general was hesitant at first, he decided he would go on one condition — that Morrieu would forgive him. This was something that Morrieu could not do. He would save him from the danger at hand, but he could not forgive what he had done. Consequently that night the hooded villagers came, burned down the cottage, and shot Engel and his wife dead.[32]

Those who watched the play left the theater wondering about this strange "forgiveness" that Engel demanded and Morrieu was unable to give him. The scriptures say: "If we confess our sins, he who is faithful and just will forgive our sins." But Morrieu could not do this.

In conclusion, Smedes closed the discussion of this play, *The Black Angel,* by citing an incident in the life of Corrie Ten Boom. She had seen the worse of the war in a Nazi prison camp. After the war she went on a speaking tour throughout Europe preaching "forgiveness" as the only solution to their present plight. She thought she was able to forgive after all these years until she spoke in Munich, Germany. After the service a man came up to her and said, "How grateful I am for your message, Fraulein… To think that, as you say, he has washed my sins away."

He put out his hand to her. Corrie found herself looking hard in the face of an old SS guard who had watched and sneered at the frightened women prisoners while they were forced to take delousing showers in front of him at the camp. It was too much for Corrie; she kept her hand by her side. She just could not shake his hand. At that moment she could not forgive. Then she breathed a silent prayer: "Jesus, I cannot forgive him. Give me your forgiveness."

After that prayer, she somehow felt forgiving, and she gradually raised her hand and took the hand of the

32. Lewis B. Smedes, *Forgive and Forget: Healing the Hurts We Don't Deserve* (New York: Harper & Row Publishers, 1984), 24-25.

man who done unimaginable things to her and other women prisoners. She was now free to make a new beginning even with this man who had done unforgivable things to women prisoners."[33]

Amen.

33. Lewis B. Smedes, *How Can It Be All Right When Everything Is All Wrong?* (Wheaton, Illinois: Harold Shaw Publishers, 1999), 60-61.

Proper 25 / Ordinary Time 30 / Pentecost 20
Luke 18:9-14

Two Contrasting Prayers

A newspaper reporter once wrote about visiting a church to hear a famous Boston preacher. Later he reported in his column about the pastoral prayer. "It was the most eloquent prayer ever offered to a Boston audience," but is it not true that prayer is to be offered to God, and to God alone?

Jesus once told a parable about two men who went to worship to pray.

If we had a helicopter in those days, we could have followed these two men as they left their respective homes. From our vantage point in the sky we would observe that the two men started out from different parts of the city but they seem to be going in the same direction. It would seem that the two men had the same destination in mind, the temple, seated high on a hill in the sacred city of Jerusalem. The two men meet at the temple steps and then go their separate ways, ostensibly to the place of prayer. The one man we were told was a Pharisee, a member of the strictest religious group in first-century Judaism. Listen as he haughtily prayed:

"God I thank you that I am not like other men…"
He then went on to tell God that he was not an extortionist, not unjust, not an adulterer, and certainly not

like this tax collector who had the audacity to come to the temple to pray. The Pharisee went on to say that he fasted twice a week and gave tithes of all he received. All of these are commendable traits; nonetheless, there seemed to be something wrong with the prayer. The Pharisee did not seem to be praying, but rather he seemed to be telling God how good he was.

Let us turn our attention to the other man who had come to worship and pray. He was a publican, or a tax collector, as the Pharisee rightly assumed. Today, people complain about paying taxes, even though they know the taxes are necessary to provide essential services expected in a progressive society. In the Palestine of Jesus' day, the tax collectors had a really bad name. The Roman occupational forces had created an intolerable situation. They had persuaded certain Jewish inhabitants to do the unpleasant, but lucrative, task of collecting taxes from their own people on behalf of the Roman government. The Roman authorities authorized a stipulated tax, and whatever amount could be collected over and above that amount could be the tax collector's money. It was a system that led to all kinds of extortion and corruption. It was little wonder that this tax collector was hated and despised by his fellow citizens. Today, we would call such people collaborators or "turncoats."

But listen to this man's prayer: "God have mercy on me, a sinner." The man had sinned, and he made no excuses. He compared him with no one but God. He threw himself entirely upon the mercy and grace of God.

Jesus concluded the story by saying, "I tell you this man (that is the tax collector) rather than the other (the Pharisee) went home justified before God."

Along this same line, Janet Ross sang another black spiritual that seems to be in the same spirit as the tax collector's prayer. Once again I have gained permission from Janet to quote her touching comments. The spiritual that Janet sang movingly was "It's me, it's me, O Lord, standing in the need of prayer." "Not my brother, not my sister..., not the preacher, not the deacon..., not my father, not my mother... not the stranger, not my neighbor." She sang this spiritual aware of the family incest she had suffered. She explained the meaning of this particular spiritual to her personally.

"The second context that is always with me when I sing these pieces — because they are sacred pieces in a sacred setting and I try to bring the depth and breadth of myself to a sacred context — is my own journey as a survivor of incest abuse. So when I sing 'I want Jesus to walk with me all along my life's journey" it is a prayer from the depths of my soul asking Jesus to walk with me through this sometimes troubling journey. But it is also a song of thanksgiving because I *know* that Jesus has walked with me every step of this journey and I have never ever been alone. It's a song of commitment. Ultimately, I choose to walk this journey with Jesus — not just by myself and not chasing someone else's approval, I choose Jesus (and you probably don't want me to get started about why and how much I love Jesus.)

"And I sing it's me, O Lord, standing in the need of prayer, not my father... but it is me, O Lord standing in the need of prayer because I need to be right with God. It's all about me. I can only be responsible for myself and my relationship with God. I can't change anyone else. I can't make someone be someone or something they are not. I can only work on my own stuff, if you will.

"I decided a long time ago that God — and only God — could deal with my father. When Jesus prayed as he was dying on the cross, 'Father, forgive them for they know what they do,' I heard: 'God, I give over to you even those who kill me. They really don't have a clue, in the depths of their being, the horror of what they are doing. So I give them to you God to forgive. They are yours to forgive. They are not mine. I felt God let me off the hook. My father belonged to God, not to me. And I know that I am in constant need of prayer to live the life of grace and forgiveness and courage and hope that I long to live.' (By the way, as I write this, one year ago today, my father died — and that's a whole other chapter of miracles and God's unfathomable, abundant love.)

"The other context that is with me, particularly when I sing these pieces as I lead worship, is that I *know* that at least 99% of the people sitting/standing singing in those pews have also had times when their journey has been difficult. I take it as a given that because they are in that worship setting that they know we're going to talk about Jesus and that they're okay with that. So I can let my hair down and belt, 'I want Jesus to walk with me.' I sing as exuberantly as I can — for them, because maybe they can't sing it quite 100% for themselves. So I try to give them permission to sing/pray intentionally: 'I want Jesus to walk with me along my life's journey. And similarly, "it's me, O Lord, standing in the need of prayer."'"[34]

Despite the fact that the black spirituals capture so poignantly the biblical understanding of prayer, yet

34. Emails from Janet Ross, November 21, 2015. Used by permission.

African-American spirituals have had a difficult time being accepted as part of Christian music in America. For example, Fisk University in Nashville, Tennessee opened its doors in 1866 after the Civil War. Within four years the university had to close, the buildings were rotting and there was not enough money to provide food for the students. George White, a music instructor, one of the white professors appointed to help at this crisis period suggested his choir could go on a few fund-raising concerts, but the board of trustees said, "No." We decided to go anyway. He selected nine students, most of them former slaves, and they started out in 1871 for a tour of the Midwest.

At Oberlin College in Ohio the National Council of Congregational Churches was meeting. There was opposition to have the black singers from Nashville perform, but George White insisted they be permitted to sing one song. The spiritual they sang was "Steal away, steal away, steal away to Jesus."

Among the delegates that day was Henry Ward Beecher, the noted pastor from Brooklyn, New York. He invited the group to sing at his Plymouth Church in Brooklyn in 1871. The Jubilee Singers, as they were known by then, received a rousing ovation. Beecher stood up afterward and stated: Ladies and gentlemen, I'm going to do what I want every person in this house to do. He turned his pockets inside out, giving all the money to the Jubilee Singers. That night the offering was $1,300. Newspapers picked up the story and soon the Jubilee Singers had engagements around the world.[35]

35. Robert J. Morgan, *Then Sings My Soul, Book 2: 150 of The World's Greatest Hymn Stories* (Nashville: Thomas Nelson Publishers, 2004), 137-139.

Later in 1872, the Jubilee Singers had the first recording of their songs. It was the beginning of African-American spirituals in the United States, and the demand remains high today.

Jesus' parable is mainly about prayer, and the black spirituals, as Janet Ross has poignantly testified to, help us to express our prayers with integrity, intensity, and spontaneity.

Amen.

All Saints Day
Luke 6:20-31

The Gigantic Reversal

It is said that one day in the House of Commons, Winston Churchill listened to a political opponent delivering a tedious, long-winded address. After half an hour, Churchill slumped in his seat and closed his eyes. Irritated, the speaker said in a loud voice, "Must you fall asleep when I am speaking?"

Without opening his eyes Churchill replied, "No, it is purely voluntary."

I trust you will not have this problem today — whether of necessity or of your own volition.

"All Saints Day is a very important day on the Christian calendar. This day reminds us of all the men and women who have gone before us, men and women of faith who have shown us the way, and we follow in their footsteps. Not only Martin Luther, John Calvin, Teresa of Avila, and Dorothy Day but also the lesser known people, everyday men and women and children who make up the Christian church in every land throughout the world. It is using the term "saint" in the sense that the apostle Paul did when he wrote that all followers of Christ were "saints." That would include not just the famous men and women of church history but ordinary people too.

The Christian year cycle used by most "mainline" churches in worship each Sunday enables the people of the congregation to reconnect with the living Christ throughout the whole year. The Christian year cycle also helps the preacher not to ride his or her "hobby horse" or favorite text, but forces him or her to preach on a variety of subjects.

The gospel passage for us today is Luke 6:20-31. The passage may be divided into two main sections: First, vv. 20-26, dealing with Luke's version of the Beatitudes on what is commonly called "The Sermon on the Plain." The second section might be titled "Loving your enemies" and contains the so-called "Golden Rule."

Luke includes four beatitudes or blessings, whereas Matthew has eight all together.

The first blessing is:

"Blessed are you who are poor, for yours is the kingdom of God."

Annie Dillard wrote in her *best*-selling book, *Pilgrim at Tinker Creek*:

"If you cultivate a healthy poverty and simplicity, so that finding a penny will literally make your day, then, since the world is in fact planted in pennies, you have with your poverty bought a lifetime of days."[36]

Jesus did not condone poverty; on the contrary, his whole ministry was committed to helping the poor. To be poor in Jesus' day meant to lack any attachment to the power structure of its day and consequently to be unable to rise above the dire circumstances in which the poor person lived.

Monika Hellwig helps us see from a different perspective the advantages there might be in being poor:

36. Annie Dillard, *Pilgrim at Tinker Creek,* (New York: Harper Perennial, 1998), 17.

1. The poor know they are in urgent need of redemption.
2. The poor know not only their dependence on God and on powerful people but also their interdependence with one another.
3. The poor rest their security not on things but on people.
4. The poor have no exaggerated sense of their own importance, and no exaggerated need of privacy.
5. The poor expect little from competition and much from cooperation.
6. The poor can distinguish between necessities and luxuries.
7. The poor can wait, because they have acquired a kind of dogged patience born of acknowledged dependence.
8. The fears of the poor are more realistic and less exaggerated, because they already know that one can survive great suffering and want.
9. When the poor have the gospel preached to them, it sounds like good news and not like a threat or a scolding.
10. The poor can respond to the call of the gospel with a certain abandonment and uncomplicated totality because they have so little to lose and are ready for anything.[37]

The second blessing is:
"Blessed are you who are hungry now, for you will be filled."

37. Philip Yancey, *The Jesus I Never Knew* (Grand Rapids, Michigan: Zondervan Publishing House, a Division of Harper Collins Publishers, 1995), 115.

People in Jesus' day knew real hunger. They probably ate meat once a week, if they were fortunate. Starvation was a fact of life for not a few people in first-century Palestine.

But there would come a day when they would be "filled." When the day of Shalom arrived they would know abundance. In the meantime, since Jesus had come, signs of his kingdom had already come, and he was motivating his followers to supply food where needed.

The third blessing is:

"Blessed are you who weep now: for you will laugh."

To weep is to know brokenness and despair, especially at the time of death. To lose someone through death was very common in Jesus' day. Of course, death is not the only cause of weeping. Just thinking about all the suffering in the world is enough to make one cry, Jesus promised to be with his disciples when they grieved, and after he left them he gave them the promise of the Holy Spirit to be with them always.

The fourth blessing is:

"Blessed are you when people hate you, and when they exclude you, revile you, and defame you on account of the son of man, rejoice in the day and leap for joy, for surely your reward is great in heaven; for that is what their ancestors did to the prophets."

Whenever we take seriously our personal commitment to Christ we receive God's greatest gift of all. After Jesus' resurrection, the church was persecuted with horrible deaths by wild animals and public burnings. Shane Stanford wrote *"Real Christianity is far from passive; it is passionate, faithful, uncomforted and, at times, dangerous. It is also the open doorway to God's kingdom, and we have been asked to make our way inside."*[38]

In the next part of this first section we have a series of four "woes" that are antithetical to the beatitudes. Keith Nickel gave us a warning, however, when he stated: ""the latter... are not offered as scare tactics to stimulate a change of behavior in the impious. They describe the opposite of kingdom-quality life. In addition, the woes, much like the beatitudes, offer assurance and encouragement to the faithful, only now it is by contrast."[39]

In the second main section, Luke 6:27-31, which we might call "Love Your Enemies" contains the so-called "Golden Rule." In this section the followers of Jesus are called upon to love their enemies. They are to do this by non-violence no matter how they are treated. Rather than take advantage of the other person, as the people of faith we should use the love ethic and passive resistance.

Philip Yancey in his best-selling book, *The Jesus I Never Knew,* in his chapter on the Beatitudes used the subtitle of "Lucky are the Unlucky"[40] to explain his understanding of the Beatitudes. Even though he used the gospel of Matthew as his basis for his study his insights were valid.

Yancey told the story of visiting the Wycliffe Bible Translators at their austere headquarters in the Arizona desert. They lived in a concrete-block building with

38. Shane Stanford, *The Eight Blessings: Rediscovering the Beatitudes* (Nashville: Abingdon Press, 2007), 128.

39. *Keith F. Nickel, Preaching the Gospel of Luke: Proclaiming God's Royal Rule* (Louisville, Kentucky: Westminster John Knox Press, 2000), 67-68.

40. Philip Yancey, *The Jesus I Never Knew,* 105.

a metal roof in preparation for living a life of hardship in some remote part of the world.

One morning Yancey went out for an early morning jog in the midst of rattlesnakes and scorpions. As he continued suddenly a shimmering resort appeared out of nowhere. He noticed the outstanding facilities of the resort including two Olympic-size swimming pools, aerobic workout rooms, a cinder jogging trail, lush gardens, a baseball diamond, soccer fields and horse stables. He learned later that these facilities belonged to a famous eating disorder clinic that catered to movie stars and famous athletes. Further, the clinic featured the latest twelve-step program techniques. The staff included a number of PhDs and MDs. Clients were charged $300 per day.

As Yancey jogged slowly back to the Wycliffe base he became sharply aware of the contrast between the two institutions. The one sought to prepare people to serve God here and in eternity, whereas the other sought to prepare people to enjoy this life. It became obvious to him which institution the world honors.[41]

Jesus embodied the former way of life, and he was prepared to face the hard truths implied in such a decision. He calls each one of us to follow in the same way.

41. Ibid., 110-111.

Proper 26 / Ordinary Time 31 / Pentecost 21
Luke 19:1-10

Out On A Sycamore Limb

Why do children love this story so much? Tom Wright offered one explanation:

"Sunday schools love Zacchaeus. At least they love to act out his story and sing about him. The little man who climbs up a tree to see Jesus provides one of the most vivid short stories in the Bible. Children can identify with Zacchaeus; they often find themselves at the back of a crowd and can't see what's going on. Many adults too, can identify with, they like to get closer to Jesus, but find it embarrassing to do so, and potentially costly."[42]

Zacchaeus lived in Jericho, "the city of palms, situated at the base of the hill leading to Jerusalem. He was taunted and hated by everyone in Jericho because he was not only a tax collector but he was the chief tax collector in the region. Fred Craddock, biblical scholar, contended that being the "chief" tax collector implicated him more deeply in the corrupt tax system of the Roman government. In a corrupt system the loftier one's position, the greater one's complicity in that system. While nothing of the private life of Zacchaeus is revealed in the story, this much we know on principle, no one can be privately righteous while participating

---

42. Tom Wright, *Luke for Everyone*, 221-222.

in and profiting from a program that robs and crushes other persons."[43]

Zacchaeus had become frightfully rich on monies "stolen" from the ordinary people of the city. Being slight of stature he could not see above the crowd who lined the street to see Jesus, "the wonder worker," who had received so much attention lately. Therefore, he devised a plan. He would climb a sycamore tree with its low-lying branches spread out in a manner that would make it easier for him to climb and see Jesus. He must have been an amusing sight, this small man known to all the people in town, propped up on a sycamore tree to see the passing parade. But Zacchaeus was not only the most notorious man in the city, he also, believe it or not, was a genuine seeker after Jesus whom he heard about so much in recent days. Even though he had obtained fabulous riches and all those riches could buy, there was something still missing in his life. Perhaps Zacchaeus had heard this man really was "a friend of tax collectors and sinners" (Luke 7:34). In spite of the embarrassment and ridicule he would get from the hometown folks, he proceeded to climb this tree and make a fool of himself.

Nonetheless, it was Zacchaeus who was picked out by Jesus to go to his house for dinner. "Hurry and come down; for I must stay at your house this day. When the people saw what Jesus was about to do, they grumbled and said, "He has gone to be the guest of one who was a sinner"(19:7).

But in all this, Zacchaeus' motives seemed to be sincere. In conversation with Jesus, he said, "Look, half of

---

43. Fred Craddock, *Interpretation: Luke, A Bible Commentary for Teaching and Preaching*, 218.

my possessions, Lord, I give to the poor, and if I have defrauded anyone of anything, I will pay back four times as much" (19:8). Levitical law demanded only that the principal amount should be paid back and "one fifth" be added to it as interest (Leviticus 6:5).

Most importantly, Zacchaeus did not give mere intellectual assent to the message of the gospel but engaged in full repentance and true faith that involved his whole person.

Unlike the rich person mentioned in chapter eighteen of the gospel of Luke who would not give up his riches, Zacchaeus was willing to give back more than the law required. Also, we know that the story of Jesus and Zacchaeus only occurs in Luke, not the other gospels.

Peter Gomes, recalling his worship in the black church in Plymouth, Massachusetts where he grew up, tells of the excitement during "offering" time. The people would get up and come to the front of the sanctuary and personally present their monies while the whole congregation was singing rousing hymns. The stewards counted the money as it was received. If not enough monies were given, the procession would begin again and the people would be asked to give until the goal had been reached. The congregation would sing again. If the amount still had not been reached, the people once again would be asked to give. The minister might say, "We need only fifteen dollars, who is willing to stand up for Jesus and give him fifteen dollars?" Only when the goal was reached would the congregation sing the doxology and a prayer of thanksgiving would conclude the service. You can imagine the excitement generated in the children who were present, as they wondered whether or not the goal would be reached?[44]

Zacchaeus, like this black church, learned the thrill in giving more than receiving. Even though he had given away most of what he thought before was most important in his life, now he counted his former prizes as insignificant in contrast to the new life he had after seeing Jesus. Now he had assurance that money could not buy.

J. Lynne Hinton, a United Church of Christ pastor living in Asheboro, North Carolina, isn't an ardent walker. One day, she walked over to see her dear friend, Nan. She and her husband had just become the proud parents of thirteen-month-old Evan. Lynne commented upon what she saw in her visit, "Evan is just learning to walk without the support of furniture or walls; he is beginning to walk completely on his own." But because the young toddler learned to walk by holding the hand of his mom or his dad, he now walks with one arm held high while he uses the other to touch or grasp whatever interests him.

It is a curious sight. Yet, you watch Evan long enough you almost believe he's really holding hands with someone taller, sturdier than he, someone you just can't see. You almost believe he is not walking alone.

"Evan's walk served to remind me what it means to 'walk before God;' it is to walk with one arm up, straight in the air, acknowledging that we need God's support, God's hand to guide us and hold us up."[45]

I don't know if Zacchaeus actually held his hand up like this after being with Jesus, but I am sure he felt

44. Peter J. Gomes, *The Good Book: Reading the Bible with Mind and Heart* (New York: William Morrow and Company, Inc., 1996), 286.

45. J. Lynne Hinton, *Meditation for Walking* (Macon, Georgia: Smyth & Helwys Publishing Inc., 1999), 43.

like someone was walking with him then, leading every step of the way.

One of my favorite Charlie Brown cartoons is the one in which Lucy and her little brother Linus are having one of their own-sided conversations: Lucy spoke: "You a doctor! Ha that's a big laugh." Lucy continues, "You could never be a doctor! You know why?" "Because you don't love mankind, that's why!"

After thinking a bit, Linus replies, I love mankind... it's people I can't stand."[46]

A lot of people are like Linus, they love mankind in the abstract but real people that is a different story. It was said of Karl Marx that he loved mankind in the abstract and developed an elaborate system for mankind, but he did not care for the ordinary person.

The case against Jesus was that he loved everyone — even those the righteous felt he should not love. He loved rich and poor alike. Being rich in itself was not necessarily bad according to Jesus, in fact in the parables of the talents and in the parable of the pounds he spoke rather favorably about the wise use of wealth. We note that Jesus did not command Zacchaeus to divest himself of his fortune, and when Zacchaeus did give in an abundant way, Jesus did not require that he give what wealth he had also. The rich person should give in proportion to his or her riches. To whom much is given, much is expected. In our first chapter, young Albert Schweitzer learned this principle and based his later life upon it. Jesus did not condemn riches, but he did see riches as a problem if not used correctly. If someone concentrated his or her power and worth in

46. Robert L. Short, *The Gospel According to Peanuts*, (Richmond, Virginia: John Knox Press, 1965), 122.

riches and did not consider others with less means, Jesus did not think this was right. They should seek a "spiritual" use for their riches.

Peter Gomes told another story from his early years of teaching at Tuskegee Institute in Alabama. During the years 1968 to 1970 he was often invited to preach in small, rural black Baptist churches in Macon County. In these churches the guest preacher was usually paid by a "love offering." Early on, Gomes refused these offerings sensing they were poor folks who could ill afford giving this money. He had a decent salary at the institute. He enjoyed giving back the offering; it made him feel superior.

Gomes mentioned this practice to the dean of women at Tuskegee, and she was not impressed. 'Who are you,' she thundered 'to refuse to accept the gift of these humble people? You have given insult by refusing them to do what they can for you.' I, for a change, was speechless. She then concluded with a phrase that will remain with me all my days. 'You will never be able to give until you learn how to be a generous receiver.' After the encounter with the Dean, Gomes never refused to accept a "love offering."[47]

One year an obituary appeared in *The New York Times*. The article was about Morris Dalmatofsky known by the people who frequented the Times Square area as "The Walking Department Store." He died Friday in his one-room apartment at 357 West 29 Street. His age was 65.

To the police and many store owners he was called Morris the peddler because he always brought with him an assortment of toothpaste, razor blades, candy,

47. Peter Gomes,*The Good Book: Reading the Bible with Mind and Heart*, 96 -101.

socks, and other small items that he resold at luncheonettes or other shops. These were his only 'offices.' He was a man of integrity. He would not overcharge for an item he sold. Nor, would he keep the change; he would not take anything he could not pay for. The article concluded by indicating a funeral service would be held that day at Gutterman's Chapel, 1970 Broadway.[48]

This man sounds to me like "a modern-day Zacchaeus who has met Jesus."

Amen.

48. Robert Raines, *Soundings*, (Waco, Texas: Word Bools, 1970), 15.

A Trick *Resurrection*

In Louisiana, a woman lies buried beneath a grove of 150-year-old oak trees in the cemetery of an Episcopal Church. Only one word is carved on her tombstone: "Waiting."

This person who died may be waiting for the resurrection of the dead, but the Sadducees who raised this question in the conversation with Jesus certainly did not believe in the resurrection. They were only trying to use a trick question about the resurrection to force Jesus into an impossible reply. In order to understand the Sadducees' question, we have to know something about Levirate marriage in the Jewish tradition.

According to Deuteronomy 25:5-10 if a brother dies it is the responsibility of another brother to take the deceased wife's as his own. The specific scripture reads as follows:

When brothers reside together, and one of them dies and has no son, the wife of the deceased shall not be married outside the family to a stranger. Her husband's brother shall go in to her, taking her in marriage and performing the duty of a husband's brother to her and the first born whom she bears shall succeed to the name of the deceased brother, so that his name is not be blotted out of Israel.

But, if the man has no desire to marry his brother's widow, then his brother's widow shall go up to the elders at the gate and say, "My husband's brother refuses to perpetuate his brother's name in Israel; he will not perform the duty of a husband's brother to me." Then the elders of the town shall summon him and speak to him. If he persists, saying "I have no desire to marry her," his brother's wife shall go up to him in the presence of the elders, and pull his sandal off his foot, spit in his face, and declare, "This is what is done to the man who does not build up his brother's house. Throughout Israel his family shall be known as the house of him whose sandal was pulled off."

In other words, the brother who refused this responsibility was given a stigma that set him apart in Israel.

The Sadducees as a group were not waiting for the resurrection of the dead; in fact, they did not believe in the resurrection of the dead. Their chief scripture was the Torah, the first five books of the Bible: Genesis, Exodus, Leviticus, Numbers, and Deuteronomy, what Christians call the Pentateuch. The Sadducees believed that there was nothing in their holy scriptures that supported the resurrection, although we shall see Jesus pointed out where the resurrection of the dead was implied in one instance.

The exact question put to Jesus by the Sadducees was this: "Teacher, Moses wrote for us that if a man dies, leaving a wife but no children the man shall marry the widow and raise up the children for his brother. Now there were seven brothers: the first married and died childless; then the second and third married her, and so in the same way all seven died childless. Finally, the woman also died. In the resurrection, therefore, whose wife will the woman be? For the seven had married her."

As was said before, the Sadducees were not serious in raising this perplexing question; it was a conundrum, only used to embarrass Jesus.

Even, the Sadducees' introduction saying, "Teacher" — a term of respect — was false. They had no respect for him. The Sadducees were a small but powerful aristocratic group, one of the religio-political parties in first century Judaism. Unlike the Pharisees who hated the Roman occupying force, the Sadducees tended to be friendly toward their conquerors.

Jesus' reply to the Sadducees was two-fold in nature. First of all he pointed out that there will be no connection between this life and the future life, in fact, there will be a radical discontinuity. Relationships won't be the same. There will be no marriage in heaven. Human existence will be more like the angels.

Second, Jesus referred to the story of Moses and the burning bush, recorded in Exodus, Chapter 3 which was part of their scriptures, the Torah. In this passage Moses speaks of the "Lord as the God of Abraham, the God of Isaac, and the God of Jacob." In other words, God is not the God of the dead, but of the living, for to God all of them are alive.

The Sadducees were speechless. They had no rebuttal. All they could say, "Teacher, you have answered well."

The name, "Sadducees" might have been derived from Zadok, the high priest under King Solomon. Besides the Pharisees and the Sadducees, other religious parties in first century Judaism included the Zealots and the Essenes. The Essenes are not mentioned in the New Testament, but they were one of the religious groups in first century Judaism; they were ascetics living outside Jerusalem waiting for the day of the Lord.

Although the resurrection was not important to the Sadducees, it was a crucial theme for Luke and the early Christian community. (See Luke, Chapter 24.)

Before elaborating on the resurrection from the dead it is essential that we make a distinction between the teaching of the immortality of the soul and the resurrection of the dead. The former is a philosophical concept that states that there is something inherent in human beings that will continue after the grave. The resurrection of the dead, on the other hand, affirms that when people die they are dead and only the power of God can restore life. That is what resurrection means.

In exploring the New Testament there seems to be two views of the resurrection of the dead. We have the teaching that when the follower of Jesus dies that the person is immediately in the presence of God. For example, in the last chapter of the book we heard Jesus say to the believing criminal alongside him on the cross, "Today, you will be with me in paradise." Also, the apostle Paul in his writing speaks of being "absent from the body and present with the Lord" (2 Corinthians 5:8).

On the other hand, the New Testament also speaks of a final resurrection of bodies at the end of time (Revelation 20:6-15.)

N. T. Wright, in his provocative and somewhat controversial book, *Surprised by Hope*, attempted to combine these two emphases when he wrote, referring to Christians: "When they speak of heaven as a postmortem destination, they seemed to regard this heavenly life as a temporary stage on the way to the eventual resurrection of the body. When Jesus told the brigand that he would join him in paradise that very day, paradise clearly could not be their ultimate destination, as Luke's next chapter made clear. Paradise was "rather" the blissful garden where God's people rest prior to the resurrection. When Jesus declared that there were many dwelling places in his father's house, the word for dwelling place is *mone*, which denotes a temporary lodging. When Paul said his desire was to "depart and be with Christ, which is far better," he was indeed thinking of a blissful life with his Lord immediately after death, but this was a prelude to the resurrection itself ... the early Christians held firmly to a two-step belief about future: first, death and whatever lies immediately beyond; second, a new bodily existence in a newly made world."[49]

Philip Jenkins, the leading expert on the emerging global Christianity, asserts: "Every Easter, more than a million ZCC pilgrims gather for several days of celebration at Zion City, the church's chief shrine in South Africa. To put this in perspective, the crowd gathered at the ZCC's pilgrimage is larger than that which greets the pope in St. Peter's Square on Easter morning."[50]

Tony Campolo told of preaching at a Good Friday service at his church. He attended a large African-American church in Philadelphia. He probably was the only white member of this essentially black inner-city church. Several preachers led the service,

49. N, T. Wright, *Surprised by Hope: Rethinking Heaven, the Resurrection, and the Mission of the Church* (New York: Harper One, An Imprint of Harper Collins Publishers, 2008), 41.

50. Peter Jenkins, *The Next Christendom: The Coming of Global Christianity* (New York: Oxford University Press, 2002), 68.

and Tony had a good feeling that he had preached one of his best sermons. No one would beat this one. But there was one more preacher to speak, an elderly black preacher, the seventh of the day. Tony said to this last preacher, "Pastor, are you going to top that?" The old man smiled and said, "Son, you just sit back, 'cause this old man is going do you in." And he did, with one line.

The old man started off softly saying, "It's Friday but Sunday's coming' '

He spoke a little louder, "It was Friday and Mary was cryin' her eyes out. The disciples were runnin' in every direction, like sheep without a shepherd. But that was Friday and Sunday's comin.'"

Some of the men we're yelling, "Keep going. Keep going."

The preacher kept going. He picked up the volume still more and shouted, "It was Friday. The cynics were lookin' at the world sayin' "As things have been they shall be." You can't change anything in this world; you can't change anything. But those cynics didn't know that it was only Friday. Sunday's comin'!"

It was Friday and on Friday Pilate thought he had washed his hands of a lot of trouble. The Pharisees were struttin' around, laughin' and jokin,' each other in the ribs. The thought they were back in charge of things, but they didn't know it was only Friday — Sundays comin'!"

The preacher worked the phrase for an hour and a half. By the time he came to the end of his message Tony said he was exhausted. At the end of his message he just yelled at the top of his lungs, *"It's Friday!"* and all five hundred of us in that church yelled back with one accord, *"but Sunday's comin!"* [51]

Amen.

51. Tony Campolo, *Let Me Tell You a Story* (Nashville: Word Publishing, 200), 213-216.

Proper 28 / Ordinary Time 33 / Pentecost 23
Luke 21:5-19

Are We Living In The Last Days?

Many people in northeast Ohio have visited the Amish Country at least once, if not numerous times. One stop they are sure to make is at Lehman's Hardware Store in Kidron, Ohio. What I have learned from my visits there is that at one time only other Amish people purchased items at the store because they were committed to using non-electrical equipment in their farming. More recently, however, a new set of clients has arrived, not counting the usual tourists. Some religious believers have the convictions that they are living in the last days. Therefore, they are getting ready for the crisis that is coming. They may need non-electrical equipment in order to survive. The owners of the Lehman store do not subscribe to this view but they are happy for their business.

Are we really living in the last days? Not a few people are fascinated with a study of the end-time. What does the gospel of Luke say about the future?

Everyone seems to be interested in the future whatever his or her background happens to be. Through the years as a pastor I have taken many of my annual study leaves at the Kirkridge Retreat Center in the beautiful Pocono Mountains in eastern Pennsylvania. Robert Raines had been director of Kirkridge for many years. One year the theme was "the future." The leader asked the participants to estimate how many years he had yet to live. The answers ranged from thirty years to five years. Those who attended this retreat were then asked to make up a menu for the rest of their lives. What do I have an appetite for? What do I want to taste again and again or for the first time? What do I not want to stomach any longer? What for me, would be a healthy diet for living?

Here are some samples from their menus:

Want to sing more. I want to visit sacred places, to complete my master's program, to visit the moon, to mentor young men, to be more playful and more prayerful. I want time for woodworking and to have a vegetable garden. I want to go to Scandinavia; I want to live in a third world country. I want to work for a year as a church or school custodian. I want to spend time at the ocean and read the lives of our country's presidents. I want to want. There is no passion in me. I'm ready to die or to be reborn. I want to become intimately familiar with a plot of wilderness for four seasons. I want to ski more: the only time I feel graceful is when I'm skiing. I want more time alone. I want to learn to play a musical instrument, and eat a hot fudge sundae without getting heartburn.[52]

What do *you* want to do with the rest of your life?

One day during Jesus' last week in Jerusalem, he and his disciples walked by the gorgeous temple in the Holy City. Someone said in awe, (It could have been one of the disciples, or possibly a tourist passing by), we are not told explicitly who it was. "Look how beautiful the temple is! King Herod had built this enormous, ornate, cream-colored temple of stone and gold in order to appease the Jewish people for whom he had responsibility under the overall supervision of the

52. Robert Raines, *A Time to Live: Seven Tasks of Creative Aging*, 160-161.

Roman occupying legions. Tourists from all over the world came to see this unique building. Construction began in 19 BC, and the building proper was completed by 9 BC. The building was totally completed in 64 AD, six years before it was destroyed by the Romans under General Titus. But the day Jesus and his disciples walked by the temple, it was a thing of beauty.

While the disciples and other tourists admired the temple, they were shocked to hear Jesus say: "As for these things that you see, the day will come when not one stone will be left upon another; all will be thrown down"(21:6). The disciples had a hard time believing his words, and they asked him, "Teacher when will this be, and what will be the sign this is about to take place?" (21:7).

Jesus responded by saying many people will come in his name purporting to know when all this will happen, but don't go after them Jesus warned. They will hear of wars and insurrections, earthquakes, famines and plagues, and other dreadful things, but the end is not near yet. Then Jesus gave them instructions about how they should respond when brought before the authorities or even cast in prison. When the time came, they would be given words to say. He then spoke of Jerusalem under siege until the Son of Man appears and their redemption draws near. Part of his reply seems to relate to what happened in 70 AD when the Roman general Titus attacked Jerusalem and destroyed the temple, but parts of it seemed to be of a later time. Whatever the setting, those who follow Jesus should prepare for that time by prayer, patience, witness, and by being alert at all times. Jesus' disciples can be assured that no matter how severe persecution might be, in the end will be ultimate victory.

Chapter 21 in the gospel of Luke is a difficult chapter to interpret; it is usually considered to be an eschatological section. Eschatology is the study of "the last things." The most eschatological book in the New Testament is the book of Revelation, the last book in the Bible. Such writings usually include an accent on symbolism, numbers, and other bizarre material.

The Jewish view of eschatology divides history into two categories: this age and the age to come. The main book in the Old Testament that has visions of the future is the book of Daniel. Other examples are eschatological writings, such as Enoch, the Ascension of Israel and Fourth Ezra which were written during the inter testament period, the four hundred years between the time the Old Testament ends and the New Testament period begins.

"The Day of the Lord" appears prior to "the age to come." It would be a time of upheaval, war, and judgment. After this dreadful day would appear "the age to come" capturing all the dreams of Israel from the beginning of their covenant relationship with God.

The Christian understanding of "the last days" may be divided in three different views of the millennium — the thousand year period when Christ reigns with his people in ultimate victory. It should be pointed out that the term *millennium* or thousand year reign is only mentioned in Chapter 20 of the book of Revelation and yet much has been written about the details of this thousand year reign by Bible commentators that do not actually appear in the Bible itself.

Three principal views of this thousand year reign are called postmillennial, premillennial, and amillennial.

The post-millennial view contends that Christ will come after the millennium begins. The kingdom of God is now being extended in the world through the preaching of the gospel. The nineteenth century was the great century of Christian missions and also the increase of benevolent societies that began to reform a variety of social ills. Optimism was in the air. Many were looking forward to a golden age of one thousand years that would climax all their efforts.

The weakness of this view was that such progress did not continue with two world wars in the next century and a giant economic depression in between, in the 1930s.

Jonathan Edwards, congregational pastor at Northampton, Massachusetts, and a leader of the Great Awakening, had a keen interest in "the last days." He set forth the stages as he saw them: 1) Christ's earthly ministry and crucifixion, ending in the destruction of Jerusalem and 'bringing the church into the glorious state of the gospel' ; 2) advancement of the church in Constantine's time, to liberty from persecution; 3) the downfall of the antichrist, now being accomplished, by the advancement of the church to the 'glorious prevalence and truth, liberty, peace, and joy which we had often read of in the prophetical parts of scripture.'"[53]

The second view is premillennialism, this is the favorite of most evangelicals in our day. This view maintains that Christ will return "before" the millennium occurs. Although many attempts to reform society have been made by those of post millennial persuasion yet, premillennialists believe the world is getting worse and worse, and later the antichrist will take over. Only

53. Ernest Lee Tuveson, *Redeemer Nation: The Idea of America's Millennial Role* (Chicago: The University of Chicago Press, 1968), 200.

the dramatic return of Christ can bring about the golden age of one thousand years of peace here on earth.

This particular view lends itself to so-called prophetic teachers setting dates when "the last days" will happen and even identifying the antichrist with certain people living in their day.

Premillennialism is a relatively late theory having been set forth by John Nelson Darby, an Englishman living in Ireland, who belonged to a small denomination known as the Plymouth Brethren whose church membership in America is about 85,000 members (Garrison Keillor, of Prairie Home Companion fame, was reared in the Plymouth Brethren church but is not now a practicing member.) Darby also applied various dispensations to his premillennialism; each dispensation had a particular title, according to Darby we are presently in the "church age" or sixth dispensation, a period marked by apostasy and the weakening of Christian morality. This period will be followed by the rapture when all saved Christians will ascend to meet Christ in the sky and be safeguarded from the Great Tribulation, a time of violence and death, to be followed by Christ's thousand years of reign on earth and his last judgment of humankind. Darby's views came to the United States at the beginning of the twentieth century. Dallas Theological Seminary in Dallas, Texas, and the Moody Bible Institute in Chicago became hotbeds of dispensational premillennialism. Even more so, in 1909 the Scofield Bible was published based upon the King James Version of the Bible, but containing in the margins the whole theory of dispensational premillennialism.

In the twentieth century advocates of this view included Hal Lindsey, Pat Robertson, and Jerry B. Jenkins and Tim LaHaye, the latter two co-authors of their highly successful *Left Behind* books and movies, both based on premillennialism. American church historian Sydney E. Ahlstrom notes that although adherents of this view claim to be literalists, dependence on highly debatable (not to say fanciful) interpretations of some obscure apocalyptic passages have led many to insist that its interpretation is anything but literal.[54]

The third view of millennalism is what might be called amillennialism. This view regards the thousand years, like other numerals in Revelation as symbolic. The millennium does not refer to a literal one thousand years but a very long time stretching from the first coming of Christ to his second coming. This is a more "realistic" view, somewhere between the optimistic view of the postmillennialist view and the pessimistic view of the premillennial view. The millennialist theory assumes that good and evil will continue until "the last days" when Christ comes again to destroy the forces of evil forever and issue in the peaceable kingdom.[55]

Each of these views has difficulties; this third one which most mainline and historic churches from the time of the Reformation adhere to this one, and it is the one that makes best sense to me. Its main drawback is that some churches treat the book of Revelation as the only book in the New Testament; followers of the amillennial view tend to neglect the book altogether and concentrate on other matters.

I heard of a group of theological students who were studying the gospel of Luke, Chapter 21 in the seminary gym when the custodian walked by, and they

54. Sydney E. Ahlstrom, A Religious History of the American People, Volume 2 (Garden City, New York: Image Books, A Division of Doubleday & Company, Inc., 1975), 281.

55. Bruce Metzger, *Breaking the Code: Understanding the Book of Revelation* (Nashville: Abingdon Press, 1993), 94-95.

thought they would have a little fun with him. They told him the eschatological passage they were studying and wondered if he could help with the interpretation. The old man looked at the passage of scripture, and then without hesitation he gave them an answer. He said the passage said, "God wins!"

This would seem to be the underlying theme of Jesus' eschatological teaching in chapter 21 of the gospel of Luke, as well as the central point of the book of Revelation. John, the author of the book, wrote in symbolic language so that the enemy, the Roman Empire, would not know what he was writing, but only those being oppressed on the mainland of Asia Minor would understand its meaning. The book was written to give hope that in the midst of their persecution, they would not give up and realize that in the end God would be victorious no matter how dark the day seems now. For us today, the same message holds true, Luke is convinced at the right time all things will be made right. We can count on it.

Amen.

Christ the King Sunday (Proper 29)
Luke 23:33-43

A Last Appeal

Robert Raines told the story of the day when a daughter was going through the things left over after her mother's death, and she found this anonymous poem:

I dreamed death came the other night.
And heaven's gates swung wide,
With kindly grace, an angel asked me inside
 And there to my astonishment,
Stood folks I'd known on earth —
Some I judged and labeled as
"Unjust" or "Little Worth."

Indignant words rose to my lips
but none were set free
For every face showed stunned surprise …
No one expected *me*![56]

I am sure that there will be surprises in the after-life. Surprises galore existed on the last day of Jesus' on the cross too. Who would have thought that a gruff centurion hardened by too many crucifixions would see this one differently? He would even confess before his fellow soldiers going about their bloody business: "Certainly this man was innocent," pointing to Jesus on the center cross.

56. Robert Raines, *A Time To Live: Seven Tasks of Creative Aging*, 187.

And what a surprise that one of the criminals on either side of Jesus should make one last appeal to him.

It was the usual practice in Jesus' day for the one being executed to carry his own cross (probably the cross-bar) to the site of crucifixion, but in Jesus' case because he had already been weakened by the savage blows of the soldiers in the royal palace, a man who had just come to Jerusalem for the feast day was forced into carrying Jesus' cross to Golgotha.

Arriving at the place of execution, the cross was laid flat on the ground. Jesus was then nailed to the cross and it was lifted up. Sometimes women came and offered wine to deaden the pain, but Jesus refused the drugged wine. Halfway up the cross was a projecting piece of wood that took the weight off the criminal or else the nail would have torn through his hands. Criminals ordinarily did not die immediately though hung on a cross; they often were left to die of hunger and of thirst, sometimes being left for a week or more. They were deliberately exposed for many days so that their plight would be an example to others not to take for granted the Roman overlords. [57]

Regarding the theological meaning of the cross, the New Testament writers used a variety of ways to explain the cross, not just one. For example, they said what happened was like:

a defendant going free,
a relationship being reconciled,
something lost, being redeemed,
a battle being won,
a final sacrifice being offered,

57. William Barclay: *The Gospel of Luke: The Daily Bible Study (Philadelphia: The Westminster Press, 1956), 297.*

so no one ever has to offer another one again.
an enemy being loved. [58]

We hear the dialogue between the two criminals. The one man on the cross next to Jesus was cynical and derided Jesus: "Are you not the Messiah? Save yourself and us."

The criminal on the other side of Jesus rebuked his partner in crime and replied, "Do you not fear God, since you are under the same sentence of condemnation? And we have been condemned justly, for we are getting what we deserve for our deeds, but this man has done nothing wrong."

Then the same criminal turned to Jesus and said, "Jesus, remember me when you come into your kingdom." Jesus answered, "Truly I tell you, today you will be with me in paradise" (23:39-43).

We don't know anything about the background of the two criminals on either side of Jesus on the cross. They might have come from broken homes, left home at an early age and engaged in minor crimes at first, and then later, more serious ones. They might even have been terrorists who followed one of the professed messiahs in that day who were committed to violent revolution. Whatever their background, now hanging on the cross, they were being taught a severe lesson. It is interesting to note that of all the gospel writers Luke was the only one to report the conversation of the penitent criminal with Jesus.

But what about the man on the center cross? He seemed innocent enough.

Although it is true that his followers believed Jesus

58. Rob Bell, *Love Wins: A Book about Heaven, Hell, and the Fate of Every Person*, 128.

to be the true Messiah, yet he was so different from the other so-called messiahs. Instead of spending time with the elite of the day — the Pharisees, the scribes and the Sadducees— this man chose to spend his time and even dined with them — the poor, the tax collectors, women, prostitutes and other "outsiders" in Israel. Jesus had announced his watchword numerous times: "The Son of Man came to seek out and save the lost" (19:10).

The two criminals next to Jesus had completely different attitudes. The one is highly critical of Jesus doubting that Jesus is the real Messiah. Something in the attitude of the other man must have sensed that Jesus was different.

Let us for a moment concentrate upon Jesus' words to the repentant criminal: "Today, you will be with me in paradise." Paradise is actually a Persian word that means "king's' garden." To be honored in ancient Persia was to be given the privilege of enjoying the king's garden.

Jesus did not first ask the criminal if he believed in the Trinity, or in any other test of faith. He didn't ask the man if he had been baptized or about his theory of the inspiration of the Bible. He simply said to the man that today he would be with Jesus in paradise. He accepted the criminal's appeal as sincere.

Jesus gave to the repentant criminal the promise that he would be with him in the afterlife, He was healing people to the very end; then, three days later Jesus does not only tell others about the life everlasting but he shows them through his own resurrection.

This year we gained a new dog friend by the name of Jake. He is a labradoodle, who has a special relationship with his owners Garry and Betty.

Adam Hamilton, in his book, *Final Words from the Cross*, shares this story:

> *There was a doctor who made house calls in the days when that was what doctors did. One day he visited a dying man, and as he went in the man's house, he left his dog on the front step. The dying man said to the doctor, "Doc, what's it going to be like — heaven — what will it be like?" At that moment the doctor's dog began to scratch at the door whimpering and whining to get in. "Do you hear that" "Yes," the man replied. The doctor continued, "That's my dog. He has never been inside your house. He doesn't know what's on the other side of the door. All he knows is that his master is in here, and if his master is in here, it must be okay.*
>
> *"The Bible is surprisingly sparse on its descriptions of heaven. The book of Revelation gives a few glimpses, but it often speaks in symbolic language we're not meant to take literally. What we do know is that Jesus describes heaven as the king's garden — paradise — and we know that he, our master, will be there, so it must be okay."*[59]

Luke has been consistent throughout his gospel, sounding his note of the universality of Jesus' message, namely that the poor, women, children, prisoners, 'lepers, all kinds of "outsiders", even a condemned criminal next to him on the cross are welcome in his kingdom. That is why the gospel of Luke is a favorite of mine. Luke sees Jesus as one who is not taken back by the "unclean" person in Israel or anywhere, but as his watchword says: "For the Son of Man came to seek out and save the lost" (19:10).

Amen.

59. Adam Hamilton, *Final Words from the Cross* (Nashville: Abingdon Press, 2011), 49.

www.ingramcontent.com/pod-product-compliance
Lightning Source LLC
Chambersburg PA
CBHW052153090426
42741CB00010B/2256